MINISTRY OF THE LAITY

MINISTRY
OF THE LAITY

James D. Anderson
Ezra Earl Jones

1817

Harper & Row, Publishers, San Francisco

Cambridge, Hagerstown, New York, Philadelphia
London, Mexico City, São Paulo, Singapore, Sydney

Acknowledgment is made for the following: excerpts from *Standing By Words*, copyright © 1983 by Wendell Berry. Published by North Point Press and reprinted by permission. All rights reserved. Excerpts from "The Rural Church in an Urban World," reprinted from the *Circuit Rider*, March 1985. Copyright © 1985 by The United Methodist Publishing House. Used by permission. Excerpts from *To Empower People* by Peter Berger and Richard John Neuhaus. Published by the American Enterprise Institute for Public Policy Research in 1977. Used by permission. Excerpts from *Two-Headed Poems*, copyright © 1978 by Margaret Atwood. Reprinted by permission of Simon & Schuster, Inc.

FIRST EDITION

Library of Congress Cataloging-in-Publication Data

Anderson, James D. (James Desmond)
    Ministry of the laity.

    Includes index.
    1. Laity.   2. Church renewal.   I. Jones, Ezra Earl.
II. Title.
BV4525.A54   1986   262'.15   84-48211
ISBN 0-06-060194-9

---

86 87 88 89 90 RRD 10 9 8 7 6 5 4 3 2 1

To Norene and Neil,
good people who have given us
invaluable counsel, insight, and support

Contents

Preface

This book is written to you—ordinary laypeople. It is for you and about your life and how you choose to live it.

It is a book with a distinct point of view, however. We write as two professional churchmen, and though we are writing chiefly for you, we are also writing about ourselves and ordinary people like us. In all likelihood you are related to and care about the church also; otherwise you would not have bought a book with this title.

However, the book is not about the church. Again—it is not about the church. It is about you—and us—and how we live. We will take a look at the contribution that the church makes to your life and that you make through the church if you participate; but remember, this is not a book about the church, or about people being good church members. It is about people and how they live.

What do people want for their lives? That depends primarily upon one's age and status in life. Youth and young adults for the most part look out upon a world that they believe will be better because of their personally having become a part of it. They want and expect to create a "good" life, be successful, be free from hunger and want, do something worthwhile, perhaps something great and lasting, and enjoy other people.

As people mature into middle and older adulthood they often, although not always, become less ambitious about the expectations of their lives and health. Comfort and security become more important. They pick up again on religious questions that first appeared during childhood and that may have been held in abeyance for a while. Who am

I? Where did I come from? What is the purpose of my life? How can I find wholeness for my life—live it in unity and conformity with nature, God, and other people?

"Everyone, at every age, is trying to make sense out of his or her life in some way." So we seek answers to these questions—the questions of faith. James W. Fowler points out that faith is "the shape of our quest for meaning. Key words are trust, loyalty, values, commitments, hopes. . . . The shape our quest for meaning takes may be religious, but it may not. . . . More fundamental are our ultimate concerns and loyalties."[1]

Perhaps you are working at your faith. You may be concerned about several aspects of your being; many are in this generation. Perhaps you have read books, taken courses, and developed your own methods to become thin, beautiful, healthy, fit, and in touch with your inner feelings. Or you are working on how to dress for success, wear the right colors, think positively, say the right things in job interviews, impress your boss, enjoy sex, overcome guilt, relate in depth with your spouse or special friend, communicate with your children, and free yourself from your parents. There are many things to consider.

But do you want to be whole—a whole person—make a contribution and be seen as a good person by those who know you? It is to this last goal that we would speak: how to be good people. While "good" is an overused, imprecise term that sometimes connotes outdated values or sentimental judgments, it points, nevertheless, to an aspect of our lives that we must develop if we want to be whole. The issue is how we make moral decisions and in general relate to other people in mutually satisfying interaction. A friend wrote recently: "I feel well if I am satisfying my physical and mental needs. I feel good if I do something for someone else."

Who helps you with the questions of faith, morality, and values? For many it has been family, teachers, friends, and maybe the church. But families are changing, relationships with teachers and friends are often fleeting or focused on other pursuits, and many do not participate in the church. This is the reason and this is the place for involving the church in the story we are telling.

The church can help people sort out and answer the questions of religion and morality. In most cases they are the same questions. Is "What does God expect of us?" a religious question or a question of morality? It is of course both. The church receives people who are searching and people for whom life is falling apart, and shares with them the stories of lives healed and redeemed. The church tells and retells the story of God intervening and interacting with creation throughout history to challenge and support. As people hear and respond, they are better prepared to face the decisions and complexities of day-to-day life.

We believe that you can be a *good* person—as well as being well, fit, thin, and all the rest. We know that being good and being well are not the same. There are myths in our culture that promise that goodness comes with inner knowledge and that knowing who you are and what you want to become brings the highest good. Such myths, however, may actually inhibit the search for fulfillment and block our efforts to find goodness.

We believe you can make moral decisions about your life. And we believe goodness is necessary to wholeness in a life. This then is a book about being good, about good people, about integrity, wholeness, and fulfillment. It is a book about the world we live in and the requirements of ethical living within that world. And it is a book about how the church, together with other primary social institutions in your community, can help.

For some the title of this book, *Ministry of the Laity*, may refer to people's involvement in the church rather than to the character of their lives. That is unfortunate, and we are writing to reinterpret the term and give it additional, if not new, meaning.

Ministry of the laity is a phrase that is a part of the

vocabulary of the Christian church. We believe it is properly defined as the outward, active, expressive life and activity of those persons who, through baptism, regard themselves as belonging to the people of God. The fact that ministry of the laity is a significant element in the Christian vocabulary means that its definition is not really intelligible until other key assumptions that are also a part of the Christian context are explained. The fact that the definition additionally implies that this ministry is largely carried out in a non-Christian context (namely the pluralistic modern world) means that another set of worldly assumptions must be invoked for the definition to be intelligible in the usual settings of modern society.

As Christians, we assume that everything that we do is ministry—is the giving of the activity of our total lives in discipleship. We further assume that the energy, the courage, the heart to engage in this ministry comes from an active living relationship with God through the Holy Spirit. As Christians, we know that our ministry is deeply flawed— that the expression of our lives can be and often is sinful, careless, and not good. Thus our ministry is acted out in the tension between the appropriation of God's forgiveness and the demand of the law to love our neighbors as ourselves. We also believe that being thoughtful, reflective, and intentional will improve the quality of our ministry.

As people who live in a turbulent, diverse, pluralistic world, we hope that what our neighbors see as the fruit of our ministry will, in their terms, be the active, expressive life of individuals who are seeking to be responsible neighbors and members of a society of good people. Judged by this standard, we do not claim to be better people, more just or loving than our non-Christian neighbors. Indeed, we find such claims to be factually wrong and harmful to the task of service to the Kingdom of God. What we do claim is that people who know themselves forgiven and the recipients of God's grace can contribute to the building of a better world.

Finally, we do look to the institution of the church to be a source of guidance in threading our way through the maze of modern life, and more importantly to provide settings of retreat and worship where we can be renewed and sustained in the task of ministry. We believe that most Christians in the United States turn to the fellowship of the local congregation for these experiences of faith development. Therefore we believe that the local church has an enormous opportunity to help its members move appropriately from the inward spiritual encounter with God's power and love to the outward expression of that love in the turmoil of our society. Thus an examination of ministry of the laity must look carefully at the practical issues of the extremely difficult task of being responsible members of society. An examination of ministry of the laity must also take into account the institution of the church as it approaches the task of faith development and as it attempts to send its members forth for fruitful service in the world.

The laity are the people—people who are not professionally trained for the church. Ministry of the laity refers to the outward, active life of baptized Christians.

We will say more about the role of the church in the ministry of the laity in our next book, to be published soon. The church is uniquely important in producing good people and building better communities. People are daily received, related to God, strengthened and developed in that relationship, and challenged to faithful living. Our goal will be to call and assist the church to do that better and for more people.

The present book, *Ministry of the Laity*, is the second in a series of volumes we are offering about the practice of ministry. Volume One, *The Management of Ministry* (San Francisco: Harper & Row, 1978) defines and analyzes the fundamental components of ministry: community, congregation, leadership and structure, and how they coalesce and interact for ministry to occur. The primary intended audience is the clergy.

This book, Volume Two, focuses on and is primarily intended for those who act in ministry—the laity. Our attempt here is to establish a vision for our lives and ministries that enables us to seek and find unity with God and other people—a unity that produces good people and communities.

Volume Three, then, which is intended for both the clergy and the laity, will explore how all we do, or do not do, in church contributes or detracts from the active, expressive life of the people of God.

We have worked together on all parts of this book over many months. Both of us have contributed ideas to every chapter. We therefore have not attempted to identify which of us is responsible for writing each chapter. When personal experience is related, it is the experience of one of us or a situation of which one of us has knowledge. In all cases we have changed names and details to protect the identities of the people involved.

James Desmond Anderson   *Ezra Earl Jones*
Washington, D.C.   *Nashville, Tennessee*

Prologue

Ben Franklin in his autobiography tells an intriguing story about trying to get practical guidance for everyday living from a preacher's sermon. Franklin's previous church experience had made him skeptical about the possibility, but he relented to go listen to a pastor and friend preach on Philippians 4:8. "Finally, brethren, whatsoever things are honest, whatsoever things are just, whatsoever things are pure, whatsoever things are lovely, whatsoever things are of good report; if there be any virtue, and if there be any praise, think on these things" (KJV). As Franklin says, "I imagined in a sermon on such a text we could not miss having some morality."[1]

Instead, what Franklin heard was a sermon on loyalty to the institution of the church with such topics as diligence in reading scripture, due respect to ordained persons, and regular attendance at public worship. In disgust Franklin set out on his own to examine the practicalities of virtue in everyday life. From his study and practice Franklin created a list of thirteen virtues—temperance, silence, order, resolution, frugality, industry, sincerity, justice, moderation, cleanliness, tranquility, chastity, and humility. In speaking of his intention to acquire the "habitude" of these virtues, Franklin says: "But on the whole, tho' I never arrived at the Perfection I had been so ambitious of obtaining, but fell far short of it, yet I was by the Endeavor a better and happier Man than I otherwise should have been, if I had not attempted it."[2]

This story is as contemporary as the computer. People in many places—both clergy and laity—are still trapped in this same cycle of frustration. Caring laity are still often forced to work out the virtues of everyday living with little guidance from the church. The reasons for this are more hidden than is generally imagined. Speaking at a national conference on work and faith in society today, the Reverend John A. Coleman, S.J., said he thinks we "are really naive about the complexities" of achieving a spirituality in the world, that working through what it genuinely means to be a Christian in the secular world is far more difficult than the church is prepared to admit.[3]

One of the results of this unadmitted complexity is that most books claiming to be on ministry of the laity are not written in the language and from the experience and perspective of everyday life, but instead are written in the language, experience, and perspective of the institutional church. As a result, they are not usually books about the practical exercise of faith in the settings of family, neighborhood, work, and society. Rather, they are addressed to the church—that is, people who actively participate in the church, and they attempt to explain why involvement by laity in the church is important and why it needs to be supported and explored. Our aim in this book is to move beyond what are actually preliminary considerations to detail the possibilities and conditions for intentional service by ordinary citizens in the fundamental arenas of everyday life. Real estate developer Robert McLean makes an important point when he says that "as lay persons we have a responsibility to write theology in the language of the particular discipline in which we are engaged."[4]

However, these preliminary considerations of why and how the institutional church can understand, support, and make provision for ministry of the laity remain important. There is much to be done even on this familiar ground.

This book is written in settings, language, and perspectives familiar to every citizen. Our hope is that they will be helpful to anyone concerned about working to make this a better society and who has a faith to sustain and enliven this work.

St. Luke's Gospel (4:18–19, RSV) tells us that Jesus was about thirty years old when he began his ministry. Upon returning to Nazareth, where he had grown up, Jesus went to the synagogue on the Sabbath and read from the prophet Isaiah a passage which he then publicly set forth as the theme of his work, or ministry.

The Spirit of the Lord is upon me,
Because he has anointed me to preach good news to the poor,
He has sent me to proclaim release to the captives,
And recovering of sight to the blind,
To set at liberty those who are oppressed,
To proclaim the acceptable year of the Lord.

Jesus' ministry was claimed within the synagogue, but it was lived out on the dusty roads and in the small villages of a remote Roman province over the next three years.

To set people free, to empower them, to give them vision are the worthy and complex goals of the church even now. These are goals that citizens of many faiths and backgrounds can embrace but which we all find difficult and troublesome in our turbulent and often bewildering world. They are goals all people can work on together, and such joint effort may be necessary if these goals are to be achieved. It is the task of the synagogue, the church, and the religious establishment in general to try to bring its members to claim and embrace a worldly spirituality, a whole way of living that is true to Jesus' prophetic words.

THE NEED TO CHANGE COURSE

Since the publication in 1958 of Hendrick Kraemer's *A Theology of the Laity*[5] and of Yves Congar's *Lay People in the Church* in 1957,[6] there has been a persistent and increasingly widespread concern in official church circles to understand and identify the nature of the ministry of the laity. Most often this activity has taken the form of conferences and study commissions in which laity and clergy discuss such things as the language difficulty with words like "laity" and "layperson" and the popular implications of someone untrained and unprofessional; the forces of secularity; the nature of vocation or call; and the ways the church helps or hinders the ministry of the laity in the world.

There has emerged from these proceedings a growing consensus that the ministry of the laity is the essence of the church. A meeting of the Commission on the Ministry of the Laity of the World Baptist Alliance in 1981 concluded that the only proper way to consider the ministry of the laity is to "think first of the whole church as the *laos*, the people of God."[7] In a similar fashion the United Church of Canada, after six official studies of the subject of ministry, agreed through General Council action in 1972 that "there is only one ministry, and that belongs to all the people of God."[8]

Some of the most significant thought and reflection has occurred in the Roman Catholic church, spurred by the forceful teachings of Vatican II. In 1977 a group of prominent Catholic clergy and laity signed the Chicago Declaration of Christian Concern, which set forth unequivocally that it is through the laity that the church speaks to, acts upon, and ministers to the world. "Without a dynamic laity conscious of its personal ministry to the world, the church, in effect does not speak or act. No amount of social action by priests or religious workers can ever be an adequate substitute for enhancing lay responsibility."[9]

The multitudinous commission reports, council declarations, and group studies developed and issued over these three decades were essentially educational and political documents that served to broaden awareness and energize networks of concerned individuals. Most of these reports and conferences dealt with the discovery or rediscovery of the same basic understanding of the nature of the church stated so clearly and firmly in Kraemer's original volume:

> The laity should therefore in principle never be appealed to with the request to be so kind and goodwilling as to help the church (nobody thinks of speaking in such a way to the minister or clergy), but simply on the basis of what they are by the nature and calling of Christ's church as the "people of God," sent into the world for witness and service. The peculiar position of the laity is that, living and moving in the context of the day-to-day world, and having literally to serve two masters and to live in two worlds (and here the "clericalized laity" belongs too), they have to affirm their divinely-ordained part as members of the church in an ever new decision of first loyalty to the Uppermost Master.[10]

Kraemer realized that only in this fashion would it be possible to regard ministry of the laity as a serious business and to generate a real and uninterrupted dialogue between the church and the world.

While much of the output of these conferences was a popular restatement of Kraemer's fundamental insight, related developments were occurring. Kraemer had commented that the primary task of the clergy is to enable the laity to fulfill their special and "inalienable ministry."[11] A substantial effort began in the 1960s to differentiate the functional roles of clergy and laity. In some quarters this task assumed particular urgency because of the frontline involvement of many clergy in the social and political struggles of the civil rights movement and opposition to the Vietnam War. One result of this clerical activism was widespread confusion for both clergy and laity over one another's responsibilities and expectations. Battlefield analogies and metaphors were commonplace. Some clergy did indeed regard themselves as directors of training camps and supply centers for the laity, whose commission it was to carry the fight to the streets and neighborhoods of their communities. Other clergy declared this strategy a failure and a copout. They did not see the laity volunteering for the mission, could not see how to support people who were not interested, and so took to the streets themselves, hoping by their bold and courageous leadership to bring the laity along behind them.

People began to talk about the clergy-lay gap, and books like Donald Smith's *Clergy in the Crossfire*[12] appeared, exploring functional role conflict and how to deal with it in the local church.

In the Winter 1967 issue of *Daedalus*, devoted to the "New Breed" of social activists in the churches and their opponents, Harvey Cox wrote that where lay control was most powerful the opposition to social action had been the most vociferous and that the battle between the "New Breed and its opponents is in no sense a battle for the freedom of laymen against a dominating clergy."[13]

In 1973 a national committee of the Episcopal church found that the single most important factor inhibiting the work of the church was the state of clergy-laity relations. By this time much of the social activist furor had begun to subside, and the evidence of the gap between clergy and laity was not so much in terms of social issues as it was in response to the question of who carries out the fundamental ministry of the church. Among the obstacles enumerated were the tendency to limit the ministry of laypeople to a kind of quasiclergy, the desire of many laity to depend on ordained persons, and the unwillingness of many clergy to let go of their more traditional authoritarian roles.[14]

Verna J. Dozier, Episcopal laywoman and Bible teacher, illustrates the issue as she quotes the comments of a friend:

It seems to me that part of the problem may lie in the failure of all of us, clergy and lay, to identify properly our various gifts and expertise. . . . Many people, my husband among them, work in the petroleum extraction industry. These people are really the "experts" on "being good stewards of the riches of creation." . . . They know intimately the blessings of creation, the problems, the economics, the how-do-you-dispose-of-waste-water-without-endangering-livestock-or-crops questions. How many clergy have ever asked their lay acquaintances anything about their work, their views, their concerns, etc., in this connection? They—AND WE—think that they, in some mystical way, I suppose—know all they need to know about the "riches of creation" and stewardship thereof. We may assume—I don't know—that if something is written in ecclesiastical language that the clergy know all about it, whether the content is something with which they are familiar or not; perhaps we assume that if something is discussed in church, that the clergy are expert (irrespective of content). I don't know. I do know that few oil men take their work problems or worries or questions to the clergy. Mostly they do the best they can, sometimes consulting each other, usually worrying alone.[15]

While all this was going on, religious sociologists were busy debating whether or not the church had any impact on the social attitudes and behaviors of its members that could not be explained by the cultural characteristics of social and economic class. The trend of these studies was to demonstrate the "ineffectiveness of the church in influencing its participants toward social change and social justice."[16]

Os Guinness reported on a *New York Times* interview in which the president of McDonald's was asked what he believed in. " 'I believe in God, the family, and McDonald's, but when I get to the office I reverse the order.' Let's hope he was being facetious, but whether he was or not he was describing what millions of Christians do every day without realizing it. As one commentator put it, 'Christianity today is privately engaging but socially irrelevant.' "[17]

The title of one study, *To Comfort and to Challenge*, came to represent the dilemma of many church leaders who recognized that the great bulk of the membership sought comfort and refreshment from the church and regarded the challenge of direct social action as "irrelevant or

superfluous."[18] Finding a balance between these poles seemed
to be a tightrope performance that could be managed by
only a small number of artists whose skills could not be
emulated. Even the three authors of the book were not able
to agree on their recommendations. Two of the three suggested that the parish should generally limit itself to the
comfort side of the equation and leave the challenge of
mobilizing lay support for social issues to other voluntary,
ecumenical, and interfaith organizations. The third author,
Benjamin Ringer, registered his disclaimer by asserting that
"even on the parish level" the church has an obligation to
take direct "partisan stands on the more morally urgent
issues of the day."[19]

While the authors of these research studies were quick to
confess that their attempts to measure such a complex phenomenon as religious experience were inadequate, they also
dispelled some of the gloom of their research by pointing
rather repeatedly to the possibility that people whose orientation was deeply spiritual and related to inner personal
religious experience seemed to be different from the usual
lay church member whose orientation was to the ideology
and authority of the institution. "In general, it may be
suggested that committed religion serves to provide (or
presupposes) enhanced personal security, self-esteem, com-
pensation, or otherwise tends to reduce the psychological
motivation prompting prejudice. It might also be held that
religious teachings of brotherhood are more attractive to or
more influential on those who are more committed."[20]

Influenced by this research and by their own experience
as deeply thoughtful social activists, many clergy like Shalem
Institute founder Tilden Edwards began to turn their attention toward a vision of spiritual development and transformation. This change was greeted with approval by many
of the major denominations whose lay ranks had been dec-
imated by the upheavals of the 1960s and who had watched
with anxious eyes the rapid growth of evangelical piety.

As the decade of the 1980s began, ministry of the laity

was once again a topic of considerable interest. It was now often described as "mutual ministry" or "shared ministry"—terms that are misleading and unhelpful. Verna Dozier tells of a seminarian who drew a visual model to portray the relationship between the ministry of laity and the ministry of clergy. His model was comprised of two overlapping circles with one circle for laity, one circle for clergy, and the overlap for what was held in common. The seminarian was able to fill the clergy circle with activities and concerns, and he managed to put something in the area of overlap. But he had to turn to Verna for help when he realized he had nothing to write in the circle for the laity.[21]

The twists and turns of recent decades had brought a widespread recognition of differentiated and complementary roles of clergy and laity. Lay participation in the governance of the institutional church had become accepted practice in both Protestant and Roman Catholic circles. But in the main, laity were still being requested to be kind and goodwilled in order to help the church. Even at mid-decade (April 1985), a pastor of a midwestern church with sixteen staff members wrote in a major church publication, "Large churches are fragile and transient. To combat the vulnerability, large churches must build the loyalty of the members. The most loyal members feel the greatest sense of ownership of church ministries."[22]

Conferences were still being held to define the meaning of the ministry of the laity, and with a few notable exceptions the vast majority of lay training programs were almost completely oriented to clergy helper and leadership roles within the institution. Applicants for seminary continue to demonstrate that they have no clear, concrete conception of what ministry means beyond ordination. A 1980 study of the United Methodist church reported that laity were used or ignored in proportion to the degree of their financial and voluntary support for clerically conceived programs. The authors expressed the need "to develop a new theological statement which values the role of the laity—in which the primary arena for ministry is in the world, not within the walls of the local church, district, or conference."[23]

Even more forceful was the thrust of the Roman Catholic Chicago Declaration, which stated that the practice of the church had actually reversed the Vatican II stress on the role of the laity in their families, neighborhoods, and communities of work, putting instead an almost exclusive emphasis upon the obligation of the laity to perform church-related duties in relief of the clergy.[24]

It is important to note that for a number of people the increased use of the laity in the pastoral functions of the church and the greater lay voice in the governance of the church have seemed like victories in the effort to assert the whole ministry of the *laos*, the people of God. They see the lay role as having changed from passive recipient to active contributor in the day-to-day service of the church. For the signers of the Chicago Declaration and for many other thoughtful people this is not progress at all. On the contrary, these are false steps representing movement in a direction away from the fundamental changes that will have to occur if the primary voice of the church to the world is to be the life and behavior of its people.

Lou Mitchell, president of TransCentury, Inc., stated his opposition forcefully: "Lay ministry begins when one recognizes the wonderment and frustration of bumping into the world and it matures with the discovery that the further one moves from the institutional church, the closer one comes to God."[25]

Verna Dozier tells us that at the point in her life where she was most unhappy with her job as a schoolteacher she was also most active in the church. She believes that she was escaping from her primary calling in the world by being in church every time the doors were open.[26]

For such critics the problem is not a matter of emphasis but of fundamental direction and orientation for one's life. They see the "gains" of greater lay involvement in church life as wrong turns that sap the energy and enthusiasm of a scarce resource, thoughtful lay leadership, using them to preserve and propagate programs conceived and run within the institution. Kraemer had warned of this very possibility in the closing pages of his 1958 volume. He knew then that "the danger is very great indeed that all the talk about a theology of the laity will, in the long run, remain an *ad hoc* construction to underpin, in theological terms, the so-called contribution which the laity can make in a time like ours, when the church in its present perplexity and predicament needs the laity so badly."[27]

Listen one more time to Verna Dozier.

Another part of the problem seems to me to lie in the virtually insatiable needs of the church itself for ministry. A Presbyterian friend remarked to me once (having given her "all" for years to the church) that the church wouldn't hesitate to ask for your last drop of blood. I concurred and repeated it to a Methodist friend, who also concurred, and added "Not only does the church ask for it, they drink it all themselves."[28]

It can be well argued that the danger has been realized. The enthusiasm and interest of thirty years' exploration and study have been channeled into a source of motivation for increasing the financial and voluntary contribution the laity make to the church. The pronouncements from the pulpit and from study groups and council committees that the laity are to be in mission in the world perform a function, but that function is chiefly one of stimulating the laity to take responsibility for the work of the church as we know it today. Rather than advancing the empowerment of the laity in their daily callings, our present course is unwittingly providing reinforcement for those practices and activities that keep the laity in their roles of bill payer, legitimizer, and enabler of institutionally oriented programs and services.

PERSPECTIVE

The matter of perspective, the point of view from which we approach an understanding of the ministry of the laity, is critically important in this discussion. There are two basic choices.

Perspective A (see Figure 1) is the stance of people who position themselves inside the institutional church and view the rest of the community from that point. Their primary identity is as church people. They use the language of the church to describe what community life should be like and what members of the church should do to or for the community. When these people leave the church to assume their roles as citizens, they are reminded by the church that they should represent the church to the community. They are in some way to be emissaries or missionaries to accomplish the church's purposes in the community. From this point of view the church stands outside the community, considers how it would like the community to be different, and then sends its members (the laity) to remake the community or to remind it how it should be structured and function.

Perspective A is also the outlook of any person whose primary identity is with a single institution, and this need not be the church. It might be the school, in which case the community would be viewed in terms of the values and goals of education. For one whose identity is with a business organization, such as the chamber of commerce, the welfare of the community would be linked with economics and business, and the special language of that area used to promote acceptance of its values and aims.

Perspective B (see Figure 2) is the position of the community citizen, the person whose primary identity is with the community and whose concern is for the society and its institutions. Such people use the language of the community to state their vision for themselves and for the others who live there. That vision may or may not be well formed; it may or may not be

Figure 1. Perspective A: Inside the Institutional Church

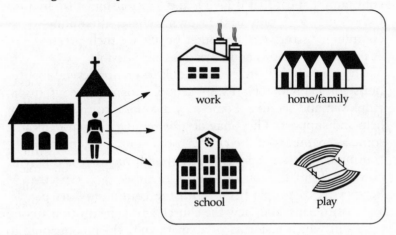

Figure 2. Perspective B: Community Citizen

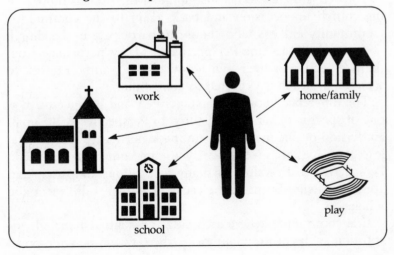

worthy or virtuous. Some may long for a good community and a community of good people. In this case they seek a community spirit that is loving and relationships that are just. Others may look only to their own welfare, attempting to use community structures and other people for their private ends. A number of visions and objectives are possible.

The community citizen may look to one or several institutions for help in their lives—school, hospital, scout troop, employer, and the like. Some may also look to the church for help and support. They may do this regularly or sporadically; some as members of the church, some not. The stance of the community citizen who also is a church member is different, however, from that of the church member in Perspective A. Perspective B people begin with the community, its people, and institutions, and view the church as one institution among others in which residents participate and which contribute to the common good. They look at the distinctive contribution the church makes to the entire community and measure its value on the basis of how the community is different because the church is there and because some of the citizens move into the church on occasion and back again to the community. Community citizens who choose to participate in the church do not usually assume Perspective A. They participate from the perspective of their own good or the common good, to which the church is expected to contribute.

The difference between Perspective A and Perspective B is one of specificity versus generality. In Perspective A the goals and vision of one institution are made normative for all, or at least its values are given priority among competing values. In Perspective B the values of many institutions and disciplines are seen as significant in the cause of human fulfillment and wholeness.

In a community where each citizen recognized a single institution as the primary authority, there would be widespread competition and discord; community life would be fragmented. On the other hand, in a community where all citizens looked toward a common vision, a commonality benefiting all, the discussion would not be among competitors but among sharers of a common vision. Everyone could join in, and in the process the institutions in which the citizens participated would benefit along with the whole community.

In our day it has become essential for church people and all people to cultivate Perspective B. Chester Williams is right when he says that in the church "the polite and often adamant refusal to return to the public arena with an intelligent presentation of the resurrection story, could mean for much of contemporary Christianity further slippage into incestuous religiosity, a situation where Christians shall be merely lovers of themselves."[29] We are convinced that churches can lead the way in facilitating this community identity, which can in turn produce more caring and just relationships for all.

It has been said that "if we start at a different place, we come out at a different place." As long as people who participate in the church begin with and focus on church life, the benefits are limited to those who "belong." If the church can begin with and focus on community life, its resources can benefit not only those who participate in the church, but all whose lives are touched as laypeople live out their lives in the community and beyond. We envision church people moving out of the churches and taking their stand in the community. We look toward community residents, church and non-church people alike, exploring together what it means to be human, to be whole people. Some will bring the insights and values of faith, some those of technology, of economics, of social service, of health, and of citizenship. The result will be good people— whole people—working together for a better community. A community perspective—a new starting place—is the call and theme of this book.

1. The Ignorance of Good and Evil

Fran looks up, suddenly intense and yet laughing, and announces that at age fifty she has finally discovered the six tasks of adult life. Her sons, her next-door neighbor, and another friend pause in their scattered discussion to focus on her words and to discern the wisdom distilled from her decades of extraordinarily heroic living. Her three teenage sons include Randy, who is severely retarded. There have been unending struggles to create adequate educational and vocational settings for him, since good ones did not exist. Fran's marriage partnership is now failing, with no villains to blame and no regrets for the joys and the pains. There is abundant grief for the loss, and yet fearful relief to have finally said it is over. She has recently founded a new business around which to structure a new career. Yet despite the depths of the wells from which it is drawn, Fran's list is surprising and quiets all who hear it.

1. To discover your contribution to the community and how you are valued by the community.
2. To find a loving, intimate relationship with an equal.
3. To discover your relationship with a higher power.
4. To discover your relationship with posterity—to your children's children.
5. To come to terms with loss and death.
6. To find out where all the socks and pencils have gone.

This list is no less precious because it doesn't come from a philosopher's musings, a poet's intuition, a theologian's doctrine, or a psychologist's research. It represents the life agenda of someone honored by those who know her as a good person. But beyond the personal considerations there is to the list a dignity, a moral legitimacy, and practical plausibility that lend their own authority. Fundamentally, Fran's list comprises the subject of this book—the struggle of an increasing number of people to understand what it means to be a good person and to contribute as a good person to a society in which good people may flourish and grow. The word "good" is carefully chosen—not "well, happy, healthy, fulfilled, actualized, centered, adjusted, assertive, successful, beautiful, prosperous, comfortable, robust, lusty, or proficient," but just "good." The other qualities are nice—most of us would take them if they came our way, but they don't add up to "good," which is in the reach of us all. "Good" cannot be defined in a few words, but it can be known and talked about.

Robert Coles, psychiatrist and author of the five-volume *Children of Crisis* series, has pointed out that popular images of the good portray it as something for the elite. He challenges this conception.

> I don't want to romanticize poverty and I don't in any way want to deny someone from a well-to-do family a rich, complicated and important moral life. But by no means do affluent circumstances guarantee a rewarding and ennobling moral or spiritual life. And by no means does poverty guarantee only a suffering and impoverished moral life. That's the minimum statement on both sides.[1]

Fran's list embraces what Coles calls moral questions. Where is my life heading? How am I choosing to lead it? What do I believe in? What meaning am I seeking in life? Many would see these as religious questions, or psychological questions, or philosophical questions. We do not disagree, but they are also moral questions. They are human questions, and they relate to how we choose to live our lives. These are questions every life answers and every person has the opportunity to address. The tasks Fran sets for herself offer little guidance about the road to prosperity or even happiness. They do set forth a moral agenda and as such speak to the unfulfilled agenda of a great mass of people.

In a recent series of Sunday morning talks to a large group of adult churchgoers in an affluent suburb of Washington, D.C., the topic was the formation of character, integrity, and values in American society. By most standards members of this group are in every way comfortable and successful. They hold positions of prestige and power in the legal, governmental, military, and high-tech culture of the city. Their questions on this day were elementary, direct, and urgent. What is happening to moral standards? What can I do about it? What is the task of the family and of the church in shaping values? There are so many different groups with such different values—how can we strengthen and clarify our own positions in the face of such confusion? Is the average citizen helpless to make a difference? What can I do?

As the discussion explored the role of the media—TV and movies in particular—in shaping values and generating meaning, one gentleman who was a military officer described his experience on the staff at ROTC camp the previous summer. Many of the students as well as many of the staff and officers had recently seen the popular film "An Officer and a Gentleman." This movie is an exciting and romantic portrayal of a young man's odyssey through naval preflight officer candidate school. It has a tough "I'll make you or break you" drill instructor, a torrid romance, a tragic suicide, a hero who sees becoming a Navy pilot as his one chance to make something of himself, rigorous physical and mental trials, and a happy ending. As the ROTC program progressed through the summer, it became obvious that many of the enrollees, and even some of the staff, had taken the movie script as their guide for what to expect and what to ask of their experience. The agenda for character development had been set on the silver screen by Hollywood. So formative was the cinema script that for many at the camp their actual experience became artificial and distorted and seemed molded to a fiction with no reality in the past or present. The officer told the discussion group how he gathered several of the students together and got them to talk about their experience, the beliefs they were testing, and the questions they were asking about the kind of life they wanted to lead. He encouraged them to begin to find and share the personal meaning of this camp experience. He was wise enough to recognize an occasion for character formation, and he provided guidance and leadership for the moral task of addressing in community the meaning and nature of their experience. He correctly perceived that many of the students, and also some of the leaders, needed help to break out of the artificiality and moral immaturity of seeking the kind of thrilling, tough, sensual, and emotionally flooded experience they had seen on the screen. They needed encouragement to move beyond thrill-seeking to take responsibility for the task of moral discovery, as Fran had so quietly and carefully done on that cold winter's evening.

In the biblical story of creation (Gen. 2:17) the tree of life and the tree of the knowledge of good and evil stand together in the Garden. This ancient story is a symbol of the perilous freedom of moral choice that is central to human life and the human condition. To live is to choose, and we may choose wrong.

"I call heaven and earth to witness against you this day, that I have set before you life and death, blessing and curse; therefore choose life that you and your descendants may live" (Deut. 30:19). An increasing number of people are coming to recognize the truth that the choice for life is a moral choice as well as a religious choice. It is a lifelong process of consciously noticing and addressing the issues of good and evil in our personal and corporate lives. It is at the point of making ethical decisions that many are brought face to face with the deeper dimensions of life, but there are conditions in the modern situation that lend new difficulty and troubling confusion to these tasks.

SYSTEMIC MORAL ILLITERACY

Americans are morally illiterate on a massive and systemic scale. If we regard as literate people who are productive and effective in their own environment, then within the moral environment of our society we are failing to produce literate citizens.[2] Moral literacy implies the capacity to read, comprehend, and act upon the signs of the times and the ability to engage in the process of moral learning and development. Good people—people with character—demonstrate both freedom and responsibility. Their lives, in all the various settings, are characterized by choices and behavior not dictated by external authority. They respond to the demands of what we used to call an informed conscience— a self-steering process tuned to the achievement of a greater good than self-gratification. Attaining and maintaining a balance between liberty and duty, between individual assertion and communal responsibility, is fundamental to the character of good people—people who are morally literate.

The concept of moral literacy puts the discussion well beyond the technicalities of professional ethicists. This is not a matter of philosophy and ethics. The issue is literacy as the basic capacity to know (in the fullest sense of the word) good and evil as they manifest themselves in our lives in society.

Eldridge Cleaver in *Soul on Ice* expressed in stark and dramatic form the cry of the morally illiterate.

After I returned to prison, I took a long look at myself and, for the first time in my life, admitted that I was wrong, that I had gone astray—I realized that no one could save me but myself. The prison authorities were both uninterested and unable to help me. I had to seek out the truth and unravel the snarled web of my motivations. I had to find out who I am and what I want to be, what type of man I should be, and what I could do to become the best of which I was capable . . . [3]

This is not the cry of a man who needs ethical training. Moreover, when Cleaver says "best," he doesn't just mean proficient, satisfied, or first, but best in the deepest moral sense of good. This is the cry of a man who is feeling the pain of ignorance—of an anguished inability to read good and evil in his own choices and in the messages of a turbulent society.

It would be a mistake to think that moral ignorance is more common in those of limited means or low estate. The Watergate affair should put that idea permanently to rest. Commenting on David Frost's famous interview with Richard Nixon, a columnist in the *New Yorker* measured the moral mood of the former president's responses and wrote:

One searched for a hint of something in [Nixon's] character, some shred of belief or awareness, that might have given him the strength and the foothold—a motive to act differently; but save for the misgiving that his strategy might backfire, no such motive was there. . . . And yet if one asked oneself what the foothold of belief might have been, there was no ready answer—only a prickling of dread.[4]

The interview made one feel that Nixon really believed and lived by his favorite quote often attributed to football coach Vince Lombardi: "Winning isn't everything; it's the only thing." The prickles of dread stem from the realization that this is all our society has to offer; there is no firmer moral foundation than the desire to win by whatever means, the only restraint being the need to avoid legal wrongdoing.

The felt pain of our moral confusion has become

widespread. Numerous articles and books, such as Christopher Lasch's _The Culture of Narcissism_, detail the crisis.[5] The broad outline of the analysis has become familiar. Traditional authoritative systems of morality have lost much of their legitimacy. Our culture, that atmosphere of meaning that we breathe in and out every day as we receive and interpret the experience of the world about us, is presenting us with multiple, diffuse, and often permissive and utilitarian moral standards. If there is any prevailing ethic, it is that of self-realization and personal fulfillment.

Someone has noted that jogging has become the modern American equivalent of good works. Until recently few disputed the health benefits of jogging. Now science has differentiated between being fit and being healthy, and indicated that jogging may or may not lead to health. It will be interesting to watch the trends of jogging in the future. Until quite recently, however, jogging had become for many a type of religion.

More and more Americans are beginning to recognize the emptiness and the pain of this situation. They are hungry for a deeper understanding of the causes of the present moral chaos. They want to know where to turn for help and guidance. They want to take the first steps toward moral literacy, and they seek a vision of a good society and their place in it. They are angry that the "Moral Majority" often seem to be the only ones using the word "moral," and they yearn for practical and concrete examples and application of morality in the everyday experiences of their lives.

Is it possible in the midst of such an immense and complex problem to find points of reference for ordinary citizens in their struggle to understand and find the good? Is there anything they can be sure is worth giving their lives to? It might be well to look first to those familiar institutions that have traditionally carried the burden of character formation: family; church and synagogue; school; and neighborhood, with its fabric of friends and associations. In the final analysis this may be the only place we can look for help.

THE FAILURE OF THE BUREAUCRATIZATION OF CHARACTER FORMATION

For the first two hundred years of American history the development of the social institutions of family, neighborhood, school, church, and volunteer association followed a strikingly similar pattern, and their concord made for a system that acted as the seedbed for character development.

There have been three major stages in this development, stages that become apparent whether we are examining American church life, the evolution of the role and function of the neighborhood, the course of public education, the provision of services to families and local area residents, or the evolution of citizen self-help movements.[6]

STAGE I.   BUILDING A COMMON COVENANT COMMUNITY

This first stage, which lasted from our nation's founding to almost the end of the nineteenth century—a little over one hundred years—was characterized by remarkable vitality and by enthusiastic citizen involvement. It amounted to a widespread social movement to develop the national infrastructure in which to realize the promise of the new world and bring about a new birth of freedom. This outpouring of energy in voluntary participation was the mutual pledging of lives, fortunes, and sacred honor Thomas Jefferson had foreseen. The citizens settled town after town, created public schools, dotted the landscape with church spires, built cities that offered a wide range of civic and social services, and blended it all into a workable social fabric.

In an exhilaration born of a sense of providential purpose

and unfettered freedom, they set up school boards, sent out circuit riders, founded voluntary organizations of every imaginable type, and wove these separate threads into communities and then into a nation. Alexis de Tocqueville, in his commentary on the formation of democracy in America, wrote that "it is incontestably true that the love and the habits of republican government in the United States were engendered in the townships and provincial assemblies."[7]

Henry Thoreau wrote in 1845 that if he were to tug a few times on the bell rope of the parish church in the center of town to signal a fire, "there is hardly a man on his farm in the outskirts of Concord—nor a boy, nor a woman—but would forsake all and follow that sound."[8]

STAGE 2. THE MOVEMENT FROM LOCAL ASSOCIATION TO PROFESSIONALIZED, NATIONAL BUREAUCRACIES

As the nineteenth century drew to a close another movement took shape, which lasted well into the middle of the twentieth century. Our local neighborhoods, voluntary small-scale associations, schools, and churches grew into national organizations. This was not just growth in size; with it came a fundamental shift in ethos. "The small community and the 'natural association' had given way to impersonal organizations with a life above that of their members."[9] Novelist Rebecca West observed that the state "had taken so much power from individuals that it did not have to consider the moral judgments of ordinary human beings."[10] Martin Marty quotes de Tocqueville: "The ominous tendency of democracies, de Tocqueville remarks, is toward elimination of all intermediate groups and voluntary associations, so that there will remain at last only the huge nation-state and a powerless mass of little subordinated individuals. This de Tocqueville called 'democratic despotism'."[11]

Public education became more and more a profession,

subject to the rational analysis of social engineers trained in the controlled conceptual language and theories of educational methodology. The church generated large national agencies whose staffs worked hard to set professional standards for the ordained ministry, missions, and congregational programs. Neighborhoods were annexed by "downtown" and absorbed into large civic entities whose power and control were in the hands of professional politicians, city managers, and other key members of the center-city hierarchy. The family became the object of attention from a whole host of social service professionals and policy planners. For some eighty or ninety years the direction seemed clear, promising, and enjoyed almost universal acceptance. More education, higher professional standards, the development of specialized knowledge, the creation of large national organizations with well-defined career tracks— these became the hallmarks, the prevailing characteristics of the whole cluster of groups and associations that had once been integral to the social, personal, and political fabric at the local level. It was a movement toward creating expertise, contained within large organizations of service providers whose professional dominion over the layperson—the ordinary citizen, the client—was manifest in the profession's language, its jargon known only to the initiated.

The nation underwent a tremendous shift in cultural perspective. There were, of course, both gains and losses from the movement, but two outcomes are of particular importance to this discussion.

First, average citizens came to see themselves as laypeople—in the sense of amateur—in almost every arena of life. Teachers know about the education of our children. Doctors know about the health of our bodies. Therapists know about the well-being of our psyches. Social workers know best how to manage family life. Clergy know about our spiritual development. The planners downtown know about our neighborhoods, so they can zone and plan how they should look and feel. The professional youth workers know how to relate best to our young people. At every turn there is someone who seems to be an expert in the very areas of life where the individual has access and opportunity and has been accustomed to exercising his or her sense of immediate responsibility.

Second, this phase of American cultural transformation lived off of the moral imperatives and values of our nation's founders. The vision that created energy and helped form vital communal bonds in our formative years was still being drawn upon, but the support and renewal of the vision—of the values that had been the foundation of the bonds of everyday life—now seemed to be in the hands of the large institutions we had created. The government, the schools, the churches—the institutions rather than the people—now seemed responsible for the moral and spiritual undergirding of everyday life. Woodrow Wilson, writing in the late 1800s, commented that people may share the prosperity that such organizations create, but they cannot initiate it.[12]

The professional-client relationship became the prevailing condition of daily life. Our industrialized mega-institutions with their corps of professionals, processes of certification, specialized vocabularies, and rationalized processes of work conformed to the norms of scientific criteria, and this brought widespread moral complacency and confident investment in the capacity of the scientific-industrial enterprise to bring about the good life. For many of the best and brightest, two new values emerged as the means of participating in the creation of a just and good society. The first was professional competence, and the second was loyal service to the institution that seemed to offer the most promise for good. The loss of personal initiative in such intimate realms as family life, personal religion, and neighborhood activity went unnoticed as initiative and individual decision making were transferred to career pursuit and to altruistic service to the corporate benefactors of our society.

These new values seemed to hold the promise of both personal, material reward and also a sense of contribution to society through helping to build (often through volunteer effort) the major institutions to serve society. From serving we moved to building institutions for service. Large corporations began to state their purpose in terms of the communal good, and their veracity was not questioned. The loss of a coherent moral vision, of a cultural story that informed the heart and gave vision to the soul was not noticed because it seemed so out of place and beside the point. Each institution, each profession, was still able to choose the fragments of the cultural inheritance that seemed appropriate and credible. The helping professions, especially law and medicine, grew in their ability to exert their specialized moral power. Medicine seemed to epitomize the capacity of reason and technology to create a polity—an organized entity with coherent philosophy, policy, and practice—that could usher in a better world. That even medicine would fail to create moral coherence for its own high priests, much less for our society, was not yet apparent. We could not see the coming moral struggles around abortion, euthanasia, organ transplants, artificial hearts, genetic manipulation, malpractice, and birth control.

Unnoticed and ignored was the degree to which this phase of bureaucratization, industrialization, and professionalization fed upon the moral capital of previous generations. People became the consumers rather than the producers of the qualities that make a society loving, just, and good. Unnoticed was the replacement of interest in virtue with an overly optimistic concern for scientific research and professional practice. All that seemed lacking was the political will to take a "Manhattan Project" approach to each of the major ills of our world. The Manhattan Project was the amassing of resources and talents to produce the first atomic bomb. That project showed, it was believed, that any problem could be solved with enough effort.

For many people this era of American life was finally to

end with the contradictions of President Johnson's gallant attempt to forge the Great Society amidst the domestic and foreign brutalities of the Vietnam War. It was at this time that a friend and colleague who had been a tireless warrior in the struggles for a better society stated flatly that he was through and that the liberal credo by which he had lived, "If we apply enough resources, we can overcome any problem," was dead. The year was 1969.

Milton Kotler, founder of the National Association of Neighborhoods, has said that "only by understanding the American city as it is today—a floundering empire, no longer in control of the neighborhoods it has annexed—can we see the force of neighborhood power in its claims for liberty."[13] His statement applies equally well to the general condition of most of our large institutions and their inability to interact with and influence the conditions of life in which the character of the citizenry is developed.

That so many of America's institutions that were born from the womb of the local community and nurtured in the cradle of active citizen involvement have become floundering empires is now widely apparent. Whether we speak of political parties, public schools, the churches, civic systems of governance, or social service agencies, the taproot is their footing in local communities, in situations where the individual can perform purposive action and express emotional allegiance within a limited and comprehensible area of public life. Divorced from this root these institutions become impersonal, ineffectual, and self-consumptive. Bureaucratic considerations and forces provide an authority structure beyond the reach of the clients and out of alignment with the purposes that originally brought life to the mission.

Participation in these large institutions and sharing in the services or benefits they provide has now become a form of serfdom. Just as the serfs of the Middle Ages gave themselves to the lord of the manor to secure for themselves a meager existence, suppliants of the institutions accept a form of servitude. The attitude is, "I'll sell my soul to the company during working hours and find my freedom and community of friends elsewhere." Some, however, are willing to lead their whole lives within the bounds of a single institution. They still retain the hope that the institution will provide the ways and means for the good life if only they invest enough energy and devotion. The institution may be the church, a corporation, or political party. More and more, however, our culture reflects the reality that with the proliferation of institutions and our multiple memberships in them, the only areas of freedom and choice that remain are the private sanctuary of the home and the crowded corridors of our shopping malls.

STAGE 3.   THE FIGHT TO REGAIN MORAL INTEGRITY

Within the last twenty-five years our institutional empires have attempted to stem the tide by becoming more grass roots in nature and less imperial in their mode of operating. Maxine Schnall, in *Limits: A Search for New Values*, suggests that "the quest for self-fulfillment has already begun, and with it the quest for a 'public value system that supports personal and social responsibility without smothering individual initiative under a juggernaut of rules.' "[14] John Naisbitt, the best-selling author of *Megatrends*, agrees with this assessment. "*Megatrends* identified a fundamental shift from a four-decade-long reliance on institutions to solve our problems to a reclamation of America's traditional sense of self-reliance. . . . Americans are showing a greater willingness to take responsibility not only for themselves but for others and for the communities in which they live and do business."[15]

So far these fairly widespread efforts at reform through grass roots contact have been quite ineffective. They are weak substitutes for visionary leadership and shared purpose in the community.

The relationship between individual and institution needs to be more closely examined. At the grass roots level is the individual with his or her unique pattern of values and needs. The institution through its executive leadership attempts to survey and engage the grass roots individual in order to understand and measure the person's attitudes, needs, and values. A mythical "typical client" is created, and the institutional staff do their best to plan in response to that "person." Through the enormous and increasingly inexpensive power of the computer it has become possible to segment the public into smaller and smaller groupings based upon a profile of attitudes, habits, and demographic factors. All major institutions in our society increasingly rely on this cycle of survey, participation, and planning in order to offer goods and services that will be used and supported. The dream of all planners is to create programs that are responsive to the needs of participants and regarded as worthwhile and therefore generate support for the institution.

While the intent of this trend to the grass roots is laudatory, its results have created further confusion in the realm of morality and character formation. There is the easy equation of a healthy organization with the gratification of member needs. The personal sense of satisfaction with the conditions of the workplace, of the organizational grouping, of the goods or services offered is scientifically sampled, scaled, and used as a barometer of well-being. Where dissatisfaction is noted the data are used to formulate new goals and programs. In this manner the needs of members are built into the planning processes of the system.

This practice has become so commonly accepted and so technologically sophisticated in its diverse applications that it is considered the normal state of affairs. Presidencies are measured on the degree of satisfaction-dissatisfaction with their policies and programs. New consumer products are designed and redesigned in reaction to market surveys. Movie scripts are altered in accord with potential viewer reaction surveys. *The Wall Street Journal* reported on the extensive market surveys conducted by MGM/UA for its film "Wargames." The plot centers on an adolescent computer whiz who is able to break into the computer of the Air Defense Command and mistakenly starts a series of events that could trigger World War III. "When research showed that female viewers were turned off by the word 'war' but could be enticed by a romantic subplot between two good-looking high school students, the romance was extended from a single episode to a running theme throughout the movie."[16] In similar fashion a catastrophic ending to the film was rejected because market research indicated few would want to see it. What matters most is not the literary and artistic intentions of a writer or the creative expression of an important moral message, but rather the reactions of the consumer and the impact on gross receipts.

Norman Lear calls this phenomenon "short-term thinking." He points to his own industry of television, and speaks of the "failure to continue traveling hopefully."

They don't ask . . . "How do I program responsibly in the long-range interest of the viewer?" They don't ask themselves how the sex and violence they program may be affecting our children. . . . The only criterion for selecting a show is how it may rate against the competition in the short term. . . . The biggest reason for the decline of public morality and personal values, not to mention our decline in technological superiority, may be American leadership's obsession with short-term thinking. When we speak of modern permissiveness, of impulsive marriages and facile divorces, of young people's inability to read and write, we're talking about a trickle-down value system that has come to consume everyone. It breeds in an atmosphere where leadership everywhere—in Congress, labor, the universities—glorifies the quick fix and refuses through cowardice or myopia to make provisions for the future.[17]

This process of measuring satisfaction is the rationalized technology to express and make plausible the cultural concept that the individual's freedom to experience is an absolute good to be pursued without restraint. We assume that a good president implies a satisfied populace, because our practices and our measurements are adjusted to what is individually gratifying rather than to what we collectively regard as right, proper, and legitimate. Indeed, the distinction between the matter and the measure is so confused that the statistical results of opinion polls become the means of legitimizing behavior. As a friend has said, "We treasure what we measure."

By measuring satisfaction we come to treasure it more highly, and that leads to more measurement, which leads to greater emphasis on rightness of individual gratification. The trend is powerfully self-reinforcing because of the investment in scientific sampling and statistical analysis. It is universally agreed that the knowledge must be valid if it is obtained through such scientific means. The way we measure enhances the worth of what we measure. In a triumph of positivism the acquisition of statistics is eventually as normative as the behavioral norms made normative by the processes of measurement, statistical portrayal, and media presentation and reinforcement.[18]

In his recent book, *New Rules*, Daniel Yankelovich considers people absorbed in a self-fulfillment quest and their use of what he calls "need language." "If you feel it is imperative to fill all your needs, and if these needs are contradictory or in conflict with those of others or simply unfillable, then frustration inevitably follows." Yankelovich believes that by "needs" many people mean "desires."

And desires are infinite. Anyone trapped in the core contradictions . . . that the self is the sum of all one's needs and desires and that one must satisfy as many of them as possible—has set himself or herself up for frustration, and sometimes worse. . . . Suppression of desires is not always bad; in fact, some suppression is required if one is to avoid becoming a blob of contradictions.[19]

Even our most value-laden institutions have failed to distinguish between what is right, proper, just, fair, and what is pleasing, gratifying, fulfilling, and reassuring. The urge to generate involvement, ownership, and participant input is enormously compelling. It seems to promise populist values, bottom-up rather than top-down communication, and the energy and commitment of a dedicated membership. These promises give the appearance of being realized often enough to reinforce the planning and decision practices.

The moral consequences are less apparent, but they need to be scrutinized. An important example is the situation of many mainline Protestant churches. Some of these institutions have been among the most enthusiastic in their attempts to use participatory processes as a solution to the accurate and widespread perception that they have become too bureaucratic and too distant from the people in their operation.

Three important considerations with moral consequences for our society have flowed from this trend.

First, these religious institutions have created a generation of leaders, clergy and lay, who measure and see their status being measured by financial receipts, attendance/ membership growth, level of program activity, and general satisfaction. In a multimedia society of large institutions, the church is increasingly perceived by its leaders as one institution among the others, competing for its share of the pie. Without deliberation church legislative bodies bestow the crown of legitimacy on such measurements and readily adopt goals and objectives based solely on these considerations.

The second point is that, more and more, both leaders and members are educated in a narrow, and hence misleading, understanding of the process of leadership. In his Pulitzer prize-winning book, James MacGregor Burns makes a distinction between transactional leadership and transformational leadership. Transactional leadership takes the form of a bargain between leader and follower in which both parties work to further the individual goals and interests of the persons or groups involved. The leader is trying to help or to satisfy the followers and they in turn, if treated fairly and responsibly, respond with their input to the bargain. Leader and follower exchange gratifications in the market-place of social interaction. Good transactional leaders quickly learn how to adapt to the changing moods of the populace or to the membership of the group in question. In contrast, transforming leadership works to "shape and alter and elevate the motives and values and goals of followers through the vital teaching role" of the leader.[20]

Both forms of leadership shape the moral climate and have moral consequences. Both have to be judged by the means and the ends pursued and advocated. But the reality is that transactional leaders tend to be judged and to judge themselves on the basis of instrumental values, on the mode of conduct, and on the means employed. Transformational leadership is more likely to be focused on ultimate values, on the ends being sought. Transactional leaders ask if they are being fair and responsive to their constituents. Transformational leaders ask if they are lifting people above self-interest toward such goals as justice and equality.

As one will readily see, transformational leaders are often charged with being elitist or rigid—even authoritarian. Some may be, even as transactional leaders may be. The charge against the former, however, often grows out of an inability to differentiate process from vision. Visions do not grow out of least common denominators or easy consensus about what people want changed. Visions grow out of the depth chambers of our consciousness. Skilled and courageous leadership is necessary to draw us out from that level. Such leaders must be capable of reaching into the depths of their own beings. Transformational leaders push people toward their central yearnings and then help them reach far enough to position those yearnings as ends to be pursued.

Both forms of leadership are necessary and important.

But too exclusive a focus on transactional leadership, on process and means, coupled with an abiding emphasis on the necessity and value of participant satisfaction lead to a condition of moral ambivalence in the leaders themselves and in the institutions to whom we look for guidance in what is right and good. Many of our religious leaders have been so schooled in the arts of transactional leadership and of sensitivity to the expressed needs of the members that they have neither the time nor the vision to understand why society questions the lack of moral vision in so many religious institutions.

The third consequence is somewhat ironic in light of the first two. Some mainline Protestant denominations have increasingly focused their moral pronouncements on global issues such as hunger and the arms race while saying little about the everyday, neighborhood-level issues that relate directly to the formation of morality in the seedbed of the family, the neighborhood, school, and local associations.

What about divorce, child abuse, the problems of the elderly, crime, and drug abuse? What about parents "being there" for their children, and children honoring and obeying their parents? What about the effects of rock music and pornography on teenagers? Who deals with the long-term cost of sexual promiscuity, cheating, and disloyalty? Who provides help in dealing with greed, anger, hate, and fear? Who talks about stewardship of money, sharing, compassion, and forgiveness?

For over thirty years the clergy of these denominations have been thoroughly schooled and trained—to the extent of creating a whole new profession of pastoral counseling— to treat the problems of living in a psychiatric mode. This has led to great gain in interpersonal competence and psychological knowledge of the clergy. As unintended consequence, it has shifted the daily habits of church life even farther away from those practices that develop everyday virtues. Courage, interpretation, and discernment are neglected. The clergy read personal, family, and neighborhood concerns largely through the lens of pastoral counseling. The laity are trained by the commonplaces of church life to rely upon the ministrations of a professional elite, which does not encourage the personal moral effort to make a full interpretation of their own immediate life situation. They are clients to be advised by their mentors. The irony is that these more personal and local issues have become the heartfelt agenda of a large segment of the American public, and the stance of the so-called "evangelical" leaders has been much more responsive to these concerns.

As a result the liberal religious establishment seems to have chosen the one position that is an offense to all but its most staunch adherents. It has abandoned the family to the therapeutic. It steadfastly ignores the moral, ethical, and lifestyle dilemmas of everyday living. It pursues a political and social agenda of issues so global and complex that most citizens despair of either comprehension or solution. Ordinary members, clergy or lay, are left to their own devices in addressing the stuff out of which they must spin the web of daily life.

The transactions between leaders and members are focused almost exclusively on matters of organization and management. An ever-elusive chase for a climate of satisfaction has preempted a core of identity based on value, belief, and integrity. Thoughtful members and citizens increasingly wonder about the attitude they should take. Many do not wish to abandon the religious institutions, but they despair of reform or renewal. They do not wish to get caught up in consuming efforts of attack or revolution against institutions that serve a real purpose, even ones that are flawed and unbending in their ways. Their simple, quiet, and persistent question has become: "Is there help somewhere—is there some person or group or organization who can point the way for good people—or people who want to be good; who cares more about a good person than a good member?"

2. The Good-People System

This year we are making nothing but elegies:
Do what you are good at,
our parents told us,
make what you know.[1]

And God saw everything that He had made and behold, it was very good. (Gen. 1:31, RSV)

Biblical scholars tell us that the word "good" can also be translated as "perfect," referring to the wholeness or propriety and harmony of the cosmos.[2] While the word "good" is a very ordinary and common word with wide usage, it points to a quality of life that is extraordinarily vivid. Try this demonstration.

Sit down in a quiet place with pencil and paper. Reflect on your life experience and identify a good person. You may think of more than one. Think of people you have known on a personal basis. This is not a test of your ability to do intellectual analysis. Do not try to set up measurable criteria. Try to let go of any concerns about what others think, just focus on your experience and use your sense of good. Rely on your intuition. A short list will emerge about which you will be confident even though you may be hard pressed to find any common characteristics. You may also be surprised at who has not made the list. You probably know some people who are quite competent— good at what they do—who have not made your list of good people. Your list may not contain anyone you would have described as successful or well-ordered and disciplined.

There are people whose performance is consistently good—even saintly—who seem untouched by ignoble purposes to the degree we have come to expect in our fellows, and whom we still will not call, in any unreserved sense, "good people." We will not so describe them when we think their virtue is blind adherence to authority training, for example—or, as one of Steinbeck's characters, merely due to lack of energy.[3]

One man included on his list a reformed drunk. He described the fellow as "stubborn, given to rather long-winded and convoluted patterns of speech and certainly not destined to rise to the top of his profession despite a somewhat eccentric brilliance." But he went on to say, "I know this man as good not because of any characteristics, traits, or labels I could use to describe him but because of what I know within because of my friendship with him." Good is a quality that can be found in a community, in a neighborhood, in a home, in a family as fully as in an individual. In the Creation story the quality of good is everywhere.

What is the quality? John Spencer points out that

in the general outlook of Western civilization goodness has been interpreted in static terms, ultimately. It has been the "right" way or the "ideal" way obligating men to follow it. Or it has been a state of existence expressed by certain virtues in the good man and in the good society. [Spencer proposes a shift in understanding so that] Goodness [is] any actual situation in which the individuals are so ordered that they enhance each other's fulfillment and at the same time increase the conditions for future goodness. . . . Community and institutions are essential to goodness.[4]

Christopher Alexander, architect, and director of the Center for Environmental Structure at the University of California, Berkeley, has studied and written extensively on the matter.

We have been taught that there is no objective difference between good buildings and bad, good towns and bad.

The fact is that the difference between a good building and a bad building, between a good town and a bad town is an objective matter. It is the difference between health and sickness, wholeness and dividedness, self-maintenance and self-destruction.

But it is easy to understand why people believe so firmly that there is no single, solid basis for the difference between good building and bad.

It happens because the single central quality which makes the difference cannot be named.[5]

Alexander prefers to say that this quality has no name because all names are too broad, too inexact to define the quality called good. We need to remember that it is a quality that cannot be captured as a formula or in a word or in a set of precepts or in a statistical set. Alexander chooses several words to point to facets of the quality, each word highlighting some of its nature but none defining it.

The good is alive, he says. All living things are alive, but we all have acquaintances who are lifeless. Some people show us what it means to have life abundant even when the circumstances of their lives are filled with tragedy and deprivation.

The good is whole, not at war with itself, somehow free of inner contradictions. The good alcoholic man has a dozen defects, but he is somehow whole.

The good is free, not forced or calculated. It has the easy, comfortable, graceful nature of a soaring bird or natural athlete. It is uncontrived and egoless. At the same time the good is delicate—the smallest of details, the most subtle difference can destroy it. The good, therefore, cannot be borrowed or copied as if it were a thing. The work of all really good craftspeople demonstrates these facets of the quality without a name.

Finally, Alexander suggests that we might call this quality eternal because it has a transcendence that sets it outside the temporal order. But here again the word fails us because the good is so ordinary, so much a part of life.

If you consider this struggle with words to describe "good," it soon becomes apparent that we can appreciate the significance and relevance of each word, not because it defines and describes the quality without a name, but because we all already understand the quality and carry the understanding in our hearts. "The search which we make for this quality in our own lives, is the central search of any person, and the crux of any individual person's story. It is the search for those moments and situations where we are most alive."[6]

A lonely divorced man told a study group at great length of his excitement and happiness because he believed he had found the woman of his dreams. However, as his story of the relationship unfolded in the succeeding weeks, one could not help coming to the inner conclusion that the relationship was not good—the nameless quality was missing. All of us have had similar experiences. We cannot really name the missing element, but we can sometimes know with great certainty that it is or is not there.

Do not be misled. Don't think for a moment that this means that good is totally a subjective matter, a question of aesthetics, of taste and style. The missing quality in the lonely man's relationship may be hidden from others, and be there nevertheless. Or he and his friend may work at and develop a relationship that grows into goodness. The central question is how to come to the knowledge of good and evil. We can be in a good building and recognize it. We can recognize good people and not know why they are good. We can get top grades in an ethics course and still not be good, or even able to discern good and evil. One thing can be said with certainty. To choose the good is to choose life, and life is always characterized by risk, ambiguity, inconsistency, and paradox. This does not mean that good is illusory, ephemeral, or unknowable—only that it is risky and difficult in a distorted world to know the good and to act with moral courage.

We know about the law of gravity, not because anyone can yet define it or quantify and objectify it, but because we experience immediately and directly its effects. Does this make the law of gravity a subjective experience of taste and style? Of course not.

Millions of dollars have been spent attempting to convince the American public that cigarette smoking is a matter of taste and style, simply a way of experiencing pleasure and making a statement about oneself. Is this message correct? Of course not. If a young woman makes a serious statement about her purpose in living, is that only a matter of taste and style? Yet, many people have learned to say yes to this question. They look at religion and philosophy and see no clear convincing guidance. The information from psychiatry and the social sciences is contradictory and confusing. At no point in contemporary culture can they find anything more than a diffuse utilitarian sense of what is fitting—that is, simply how to "fit in" with the institutional demands of the many organizations of which they are a part. The cost for many is a deep sense of moral unrest. Many conclude that in the face of so many alternatives, some of which may be better or worse than others, the only way to shape one's personal story is by listening to one's own feelings and sense of personal well-being.

Quite the opposite is true. The good is knowable and achievable even though it cannot be captured in a formula or dispensed by authority or by decree. In our climate there is no way to discover the good and then let one's life be determined by it. There would be no way to discover the law of gravity living in a weightless environment. It might be possible to know the good if we were all good and living in a good world. As it is, we come to the knowledge of the good to the degree we participate in it.

A first step in the quest could be to clear away some cultural debris. The modern revulsion at moral ostentation is an obsolete relic from past autocratic and theocratic institutional imperialism. A parish church in Sweden has records dating back to the early 1600s. Until very recently the established church acted as census keeper for the Swedish state and preserved the demographic records. The parish ledgers have all the expected entries for births, deaths, baptisms, and marriages; but these ancient rolls also have many specific comments on the moral character of the people. It is recorded that Mr. So-and-So did not pay his debts in a timely fashion and was not a trustworthy person. Reading such judgments makes it easy to appreciate how oppressive the pretentious moral authority of a theocracy could be. In the case of morality there is no golden past to return to.

The peculiar American tendency to think of morality solely in terms of sexual conduct and of ethics as the public behavior of individuals with regard to truth in financial matters is a manifestation of our moral illiteracy. This narrow and largely passive approach to questions of good and evil in the context of daily living is in large measure attributable to the long-term impact of the intervention into and domination of public life by specialized and professionalized bureaucracies. A sense of honest caring, an informed heart, a concern for the consequences of our actions, and the capacity to offer service to others are possible only when we believe that our actions make a difference. Cultivation of these qualities also requires a common vocabulary to describe our situation and a sense that our lives are embedded in a coherent public community.

The growth and proliferation of professionalized services with bureaucratized methods and specialized vocabularies create a culture that transmits the message that only the expert knows enough to act in the public good, to be of help or service. The laity in the church are reluctant to move boldly in their personal ministries except as directed by the clergy. Such everyday problems as the education of children, the state of life in the neighborhood, the dilemmas of the marriage relationship, or even one's most personal aspirations have increasingly become the province of the trained expert. Our culture is deeply infected with the positivist concept that the solution to social problems rests in the hands of the dedicated professional. We try to find a right answer but do not know how to find the good answer.

In such a society everyone is a bumbling amateur most of the time and in the most vital areas of living. Even the experts are trapped, for their competence is also specialized, leaving them amateurs in all other areas. Is it really an elegy when we do only what we are good at and make only what we know? It is more of an epitaph. How can we possess specialized "competence" and do only what we are good at and make only what we know?

The promise of the social sciences has been that they would tell us how to live in a right and proper manner, as if there were a technique, a method, for fixing human problems. Words outside their professional reference have no worth, words of the heart like "honor" and "integrity" have been dropped from the discourse. Such words are regarded as embarrassments, reminders of some prescientific land of dungeons and dragons. They no longer evoke concrete images for practical application. Without personal accountability the moral senses atrophy, and due to the interdependence of the several processes of moral development the conditions that create moral courage and sensitivity also wither.

If this examination of the nature of goodness and virtue proves anything it is that we must attend with care to what produces good people. Even if we cannot define "the good," we can talk about it, and we can observe how people we know as good seem to get that way. Virtue and goodness are public matters and belong to the people. Their subject matter is not the property of any institution or any profession. They belong to all of us who have a concern for our world and our place in it—to any who embark on Eldridge Cleaver's search "to find out who I am and what I want to be, what type of man I should be." Ethics, morality, virtue, and all that it means to be good cannot be abstracted from the narrative of one's life. And the narrative, the living story of any person's life, cannot be abstracted from the community of persons who make up the seedbed in which character and virtue are formed. We must have a "common history or community sufficient to provide us with the resources necessary to make our lives our own."[7]

A common history provides a common vocabulary, a pattern of what has been valued and found worthwhile. It also provides a personal sense of being able to contribute to that history through the consequences of our everyday activity. Good people produce good communities and good communities produce good people. To discover your contribution to the community and how you are valued by the community requires mutual discourse and cooperation and an active involvement in concerns larger than one's private existence. It means knowing that our actions do have consequences, for others as well as ourselves. "One's actions can sometimes irrevocably determine the destiny of others; the mistakes one makes are often transmuted directly into other's pain." Peter Marin writes out of his extended work with Vietnam veterans and sees this as the ethical lesson of moral pain. It is a lesson he suggests all persons could know if they would carefully attend the consequences of their actions.[8]

Therapeutic techniques do not cure moral pain, nor can it be avoided by following absolutist rules imposed by external direction. A knowledge of good and evil cannot be achieved through an unbridled exercise of individual freedom of choice. Taking possession of one's own life, coming fully alive, is a demanding enterprise hammered out on the pathways and in the patterns of living one has created. There is an act of obedience involved in the knowledge of good and evil, an obedience to the call to engage in the struggle for a humane and just society.

Joan is a young woman who does considerable work with older people and serves on the board of a congregant housing facility for the elderly. Her board activities have led her to ask what she calls the quality-of-life question. What is it about the quality that makes such housing a good or a bad place for people to live? She believes she has a moral responsibility for the well-being of the residents, but she has noticed a reluctance in her fellow trustees to consider such quality-of-life issues. As she puts it, most of the board feel they are discharging their responsibility if they see to it that the residence is meeting legal requirements and conforming to the many regulations imposed by the federal government. Some board members have indicated they consider her concern peripheral and irrelevant to the primary work of the board. The professional administrator of the residence considers her questions soft and lacking in scientific or professional data and hence unworthy of attention. Other board members, who take their cues from the professional staff, think that she is overstepping the bounds of her competence when she addresses such issues. Joan has pursued the research literature with diligence, reading numerous studies on quality of life, contacting professional associations and consultants in the field of elderly housing. She has learned that the question of what makes a good or bad environment for seasoned citizens is enormously complex. There is a fair amount of careful research, but for every generalization there seems to be a hundred qualifications. Her search for hard, irrefutable, scientific methods and findings with which to convince other trustees to pay attention and take action has failed. She has come to understand that in the present state of affairs it is impossible to produce a research study offering a definitive, clear-cut reading on the good and bad aspects of the housing environment. But, more importantly, she has come to realize that this does not mean that she does not know and cannot act in the situation. The very urgency of her quest has arisen from a certainty that some aspects of life in the residence are good and others are not good.

She sensed, for example, that the initiative and leadership some residents took to organize shopping trips and other excursions was enormously helpful for themselves and others. They could take responsibility for themselves. On the other hand, she found that many residents believed if they did not "behave," the administration would put them out on the street. One of her findings is positive; the other is negative. One shows how initiative can have good effect; the other how initiative can be dampened. She learned that, in this case at least, administrators want residents to be docile and uncomplaining.

Joan's knowledge came from her concrete experience with the residents and in the facility. This knowledge was not based on scholarly theory, but it was knowledge that required her to exercise initiative and leadership in her struggle to see that such issues were addressed and not lost.

This rather everyday story is important because it contains the elements that complicate the modern moral situation:

- passive deference to the authority of professionals
- unexamined and undue legitimacy granted to positivist assumptions and "objective knowledge" about how we know what is good or bad
- interpretations of moral responsibility as conforming to the minimum requirements of the law
- the moral dignity and courage of an individual unwilling to be satisfied with narrow "professional" interpretations
- purposeful and thoughtful participation in the day-to-day business of determining what is good

Wendell Berry, poet, philosopher, farmer, has suggested that we need to give up our usual pursuit of "informed decisions," decisions supported by sufficient objective information, as a guide for action in our public and private lives. Using marriage as an example, he points out that one never knows enough to commit fully to anyone or anything—or even to make any important decision. He does suggest that our decisions can be informed and our commitments strengthened "by those patterns of value and restraint, principle and expectation, memory, familiarity, and understanding that, inwardly, add up to character and, outwardly, to culture. Because of these patterns, and only because of them, we are not alone in the bewilderments of the human condition and human love, but have the company and comfort of the best of our kind, living and dead."[9]

So we see that there is a circularity to the good—we become good within good communities, and those communities become good as we participate in making them good. It is from this perspective that Christian ethicist Paul Lehmann defines conscience as an action, an action that "expresses and exposes the connection between the knowledge of good and evil as the environment of humanization and the obedient response to this environment."[10]

This essential and indivisible interdependence between knowing and doing, between the individual and the community, between personal action and public patterns, is the only path by which we can begin to discover what it means to be good. Why these elements are an integrated whole and cannot be broken apart is part of the definition of a system.

THE NATURE OF A SYSTEM

In the public media we talk of civic responsibility and public service. In religious circles we talk of the ministry of the laity, of outreach, and of social witness. In all quarters there is concern about increased violence and crime and about the loss of a sense of a humane purpose and common decency. Religious institutions continue to search for ways of empowering their members to take action in building a just and moral society. Service clubs, the political parties, and a wide variety of national associations, such as Common Cause and the League of Women Voters, encourage a commitment to the large concerns of public life.

Despite this common effort and intent few seem to recognize that all these institutions and organizations are struggling with the same concern. The problem that we are dealing with is a hydra-headed, many-tentacled monster of our own creation, in which each institution is trying to grab onto the tentacle closest to its interests. The true dimensions of the monster remain dangerously hidden. The consequences of this narrow and myopic view are profound and discouraging.

Who is to blame for this state of affairs? Is it the church? Is it the medical profession? Are lawyers or social workers the ones to blame for civic apathy, racial intolerance, and narrow self-interest? At this level the questions have an obvious dead-end absurdity, and they always will if our discussions of the problem start from a narrow institutional definition that does a disservice to all concerned.

Dorothy Day, server of the poor in New York's Bowery for a half-century, wrote in the mid-1950s that we were becoming a nation of institutions where state and welfare organizations were rapidly replacing personal and individual responsibility for the good of society, and as a consequence our attention and resources were being focused on and channeled into these institutions. Today the shift and the loss are obvious, but blaming our institutions for the problem only makes things worse. To put all the blame on the institutions is to continue in the path of nonresponsibility that has gotten us where we are. At bottom, the problem of lay ministry is not a problem of the institutional church but rather a problem of how to be good in this society.

As a first practical step, each of us might strive for an informed awareness of the good-people problem. There are no institutions in which to hide, no moral bomb shelters to shield us from the issue of knowing good and evil. Your moral literacy is your responsibility.

This probe is to determine what it takes for a society to produce good people. What does it mean to say that it is so complex and elusive a set of interrelated problems that they merge to form a system—a system too large to be owned by any one group or institution or defined by any set of professional terminology?

"System" is an important word for explaining the extraordinary complexity we are dealing with, and it is important to understand its meaning. Webster defines it as an "assemblage of objects united by some form of regular interaction, combined so as to form an integral whole." We use the word in this sense when speaking of the digestive system or a transportation system. However, most of us are not accustomed to looking at the world from a systems perspective. We seem to favor the form of intellectual analysis that takes things apart, dissects things to find out what they are made of. When we encounter a problem we commonly try to break it down to identify the separate elements and thus understand and solve it. This approach does not work on the good-people problem.

Systems thinking focuses on what holds things together and on the nature of the integral whole rather than the pile of separate parts. It takes some intellectual effort to see this critical distinction. Many homes have an air-conditioning system. This system has numerous components: thermostat, compressor, circulating fan, cooling fan, filter, and so on. When these parts are properly organized, they function together to cool the house, but the cooling is dependent upon the precise, regular interaction of the parts. If anything disrupts the proper arrangement the interaction breaks down and the parts are useless.

When something is made up of many parts but it does not matter how the parts are arranged, that does not constitute a system, only a pile, a heap of objects. One may have a great many books in piles, on shelves, under the bed, in the attic, in the bedroom, in the living room, and in the basement. Periodically one may arrange the piles, remove old books, add new ones. This constitutes only piles of books, not a library system. A system would require a card catalog, a filing code, and an organized plan for locating the books. In any arrangement the piles of books will still be useful. Interference with an air-conditioning system will render it useless.

One may sell books from the piles or give them away as interests change. It is another matter to sell or give away an air-conditioning system. The system is tailored to fit a particular home. The duct work has a certain size and shape. The capacity of the system is suited to the volume and location of the house. The air-conditioning system is not independent. Without a complementary electrical system it would not operate.

This idea of system may help us understand the good-people system, especially in view of the fact that good people produce good communities and good communities produce good people.

GOOD PEOPLE AND A GOOD EARTH

Morality and goodness do not involve only people, the natural environment is also involved. Too often the created and the natural environment are viewed as neutral background for the real drama of human interaction. We have discovered this is not true. Expediency and exploitation have been too common in our relationship to the natural order. We are now learning to our sorrow just how complex the total system is. There is dramatic proof that everything is connected with everything else. No area is so remote, so isolated, that toxic wastes can be dumped without their poisons having farflung consequences throughout the natural system.

In the final pages of *Sand County Almanac*, Aldo Leopold wrote that

an ethic, ecologically, is a limitation on freedom of action in the struggle for existence. An ethic, philosophically is a differentiation of social from antisocial conduct. These are two definitions of one thing. . . . Ethics so far evolved rests upon a single premise: that the individual is a member of a community of interdependent parts.[11]

A land ethic and a social ethic are the same because, finally, our interdependence makes us one. There is no way to get away from the consequences of what we build, what we do to the natural world, or what it does to us. We used to think that dilution was the solution to pollution. Now we know that the effects of the pollution will eventually and inevitably ripple through the ecosystem and make their way back to haunt us. Our experiential ignorance of this interdependence of the human and the natural may destroy us.

In one fifty-year-old neighborhood a church was erected at the "entrance" to the neighborhood in the first few years of the community's development. The building included inviting, light-filled classrooms and had an adjacent playground. Before long a weekday preschool was organized on a cooperative basis by parents in the church and the community. Every morning for over three decades that building and its play yard have been a beehive of activity visible to all. Building, school, and playground worked together to create visible patterns of happy adult-child interaction at the very doorstep of the community. The network of parents, nurtured by their involvement in the cooperative management and operation of the school, became a veritable training camp for leadership in all aspects of citizen involvement throughout the city. School board, city council, parent-teacher groups, and community action groups invariably count among their leaders parent graduates of this small cooperative neighborhood preschool.

In the last few years the influence of the school has waned. New people in the neighborhood were less aware of its existence. A new pastor who seemed less community oriented had come to the church. More and more the church seemed to be retreating into a private sanctuary for its members. Then a few months ago the coop preschool announced that it was raising money and enlisting volunteer help and contributions to build a new playscape on their schoolyard.

Several weeks passed with a steady stream of announce-ments, the creation of a colorful sign at the church describ-ing progress on this neighborhood project, and a wonderful buzz of conversation about the playscape became a part of every neighborhood meeting or encounter. A long list of people and organizations contributed money, time, tools, and materials to the playscape, which was finally erected in a three-day burst of energy from a swarm of volunteers. The playscape itself is a marvel. Its swings and slides are connected by walkways, tunnels, and platforms at various heights in ways that evoke images of space rockets and clipper ships. Now there is seldom a day that the playscape is not covered with crawling, climbing, swinging, delighted children. Everyone in the neighborhood once again knows about the cooperative preschool, and many now know one another a little better. One small but vital link in the inter-dependence of this community has been renewed and rebuilt.

It might be possible to do a million-dollar research study to demonstrate the impact of the playscape project on the quality of life in the neighborhood. An even more expen-sive study might establish some correlations between the program of the school, the community leadership of the parents, and the nature and location of the building. But these studies, like some of the early environmental studies that spent millions to prove that dumping toxic waste in our rivers and waters did indeed damage the environment, would only prove what we already know.

We are all interconnected. Within the delicate balance of the intricate moral ecology that allows good people to grow and flourish, that playscape is creating patterns of living that are healthy and nourishing. The parents, the children, the play yard, the patterns of life established in and around the building are all essential parts of a web of good life in this community. A true knowledge of good and evil re-quires experiential recognition of this interdependence. From recognition can come the activity of a social conscience in those actions that embody love for others and respect for a good environment.

Maintaining a good environment for your apartment, your home, your neighborhood is as much an issue morally and ecologically as the dumping of toxic waste in our rivers and streams. There is finally only one ecosystem on this great planet, and each of us has a moral responsibility to work for its health. The preservation of an urban playscape can be as important as the preservation of a beautiful and fertile woodland marsh. An ethical relationship to our world begins with those people and places we can see, feel, know, love, and respect. A land ethic and a people ethic are the same thing. Respect for one is finally respect for the other. Parents who maintain even the humblest of homes with care and respect make a major contribution to the quality of the lives of good people and what we are calling the good-people system.

A close friend tells the story of a good person he does not even know. He had stopped by his office for a few minutes early one Sunday morning in the spring. As he glanced out the window he noticed a young woman walking purposefully in the direction of a church three blocks ahead. She was carrying her purse, a Bible, and a paper sack. He assumed that she was a student from the large university nearby. He watched her in amazement, for as she walked, she stopped frequently to pick up pieces of trash that had been left on or around the sidewalk. Her sack was already almost full.

Why was she doing this? It clearly was not her duty. She would not be paid as the regular custodians would who have that job on weekdays. He thought of going outside to ask her and to thank her, but did not. He was in a hurry to join his family for church services and decided that perhaps he would see her again. He never did, but he continues to wonder about her. She must be a caring person—a good person. What did her parents and teachers do in earlier days that led to this? Had her church influenced her to care for the community in this way? Would anybody else ever know that she did this?

Another friend tells a contrasting story. One afternoon in October he was driving along the beautiful Eastern shore of Maryland on a road that curved gently through fields of stubbled corn and seemed to be a path of serenity. As he rounded a curve and went over a slight rise his attention shifted from a long vee formation of Canadian geese to a large pick-up truck just entering the highway. He slowed to give room and then settled into a comfortable pace behind this familiar rural vehicle. Abruptly, from the side window of the truck, a beer can was launched into the grass and vines along the road. Then suddenly a large paper sack was ejected from the truck, cartwheeling along the shoulder of the road and discharging fast-food containers and paper cups. By now he was angry and without thought leaned on the horn to let the truck's inhabitants know they were not alone. Then his well-schooled sense of urban caution took over, and he remembered that he was on a sparsely traveled road and that there were three discourteous lawbreakers riding in the truck ahead. He suddenly felt alone and afraid.

Littering as an everyday act of ecological violence doesn't just break the law or add a few cents to our tax burden for the clean-up of visual pollution. It is an everyday action that tears the moral fabric and harms the proper functioning of the good-people system. The ethic that informs our relationship to the environment is eventually the same ethic that informs the relationship between an individual and society.

THE GOOD-PEOPLE SYSTEM

The good-people system (see Figure 3) is made up of individuals grouped together in families, the neighborhood or small community where they live, the larger national and world society on which they depend for survival, organizations and institutions in which they participate, and the natural order. Families are basic to the good-people system. New lives are conceived there, given identity there, and their characters and personalities are formed there. The neighborhood is the arena in which people are able to test their individuality and personhood in an open setting—to make friends with unattached others and explore peer relationships. In the small community multiple pairings and groupings offer opportunities for learning how to live and the rules for doing so in a way that produces pleasure rather than pain.

The larger society cannot be ignored, even at an early age, and becomes increasingly more significant as time

Figure 3. Living Interconnected Lives

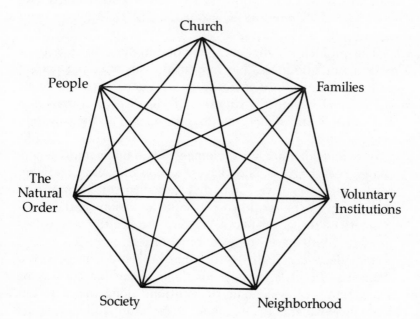

goes by. The city, state, or nation confers citizen status with its rights and privileges, and exacts duties that are voluntary only to a limited degree. Both community and large-scale institutions offer themselves and their services for our benefit and our support and allegiance. The world around us becomes part of us and we part of it as we sojourn together through the seasons.

The problem for the good-people system is how to live well: How to live whole. How to take from the system, but not take too much; and how to give back to it; how to enhance and build the culture even as we participate in its fruits; how to contribute of ourselves as we receive others and the gifts they offer.

People like Fran, who figured out the core tasks of her adult life, and Joan, who sought to go beyond rules and legalities to the quality of life issues at the home for the elderly, are really not so different from the rest of us. They, and we, want to be good, with all that good entails. We want the challenge and deep satisfaction that comes from meeting it.

The problem is that one cannot purchase or develop a pattern for goodness. No institution can offer the perfect plan. The process of learning to be good or trying to be good involves more than oneself. It involves interaction with people and structures that are related and yet beyond one's control.

Fran and Joan are wise women. They understand where the journey begins. They have a vision of what they want to do with their lives, and they can then test their vision as they act in the world to play out the vision. If the components of the good-people system are healthy and working, they will have ample opportunities to act it out and test it effectively. If this system has broken down, however, there may be little support for them. Their search may be wide; they may join many institutions along the way; but learning what it is to be good—to be a human being—and to support others as they try can be a lonely and disconcerting quest in a disrupted system.

This is especially true in our society because we have long neglected the upkeep of the good-people system. Sever the link between home, school, church, neighborhood, and community institutions, and we destroy the places and relationships where vision is formed and acted out in generative and supportive ways. Distort the link between these fundamental units, the larger society, and the natural order, and we interdict the effective functioning of the good-people system. The result is domination rather than the interdependence necessary for moral living; training for servitude rather than for free and open participation and growth.

How shall we go about repairing the good-people system? There are no experts on goodness and no available instructions of how to be good. But there is hope, and it lies in the ability of any individual or group of people to begin, however slowly and tentatively, the task of refocusing and reshaping the institutions and structures of our communities around the vision and goals of supporting the quest of people to be good. Family life has been broken by changes in life patterns and life commitments. Schools have become wholesale distributors of information rather than learning centers. The environment has been damaged by unthinking and uncaring people who have been shortsighted, while business and industry have increasingly defined their responsibilities to provide profit for stockholders rather than jobs and economic stability for communities. Neighborhoods have turned into bedroom settlements— places to sleep instead of vibrant arenas to support life. But families, schools, neighborhoods, businesses, and the environment can be remade and refocused. The vital substructures may still be in place.

And then there is the church. In too many places it has made the same mistakes and listened to the same false promises as the other parts of the good-people system. It has lost its vision of more loving communities and turned inward. But the church can refind its task and its life too. As Christians we still believe, or we say we do, that it is the task of the church to help people achieve balance and wholeness in their lives, and that includes moral development and virtuous living. It is the particular role of the church to help people live good lives and to help them test the quality of their lives again and again as they return for worship and nurture. And as Christians we believe that when people act out their faith in God and in God's goodness they do so in the trust that God is with them. This is the claim of the crucifixion and the resurrection.

The church alone cannot rebuild the social fabric of the breadth of our lives. It can, however, rediscover its purpose in the community for all the people there and at the same time model and call the whole system to account. The call is for right and properly harmonious relationships among all who call a community theirs—people, places, and institutions. The result will be good people and good communities.

INTERDEPENDENCE AND A SENSE OF DUTY

Amitai Etzioni describes two different sources of human motivation—satisfaction and legitimacy—as means of examining the basic forms of interaction between an individual and a society. Etzioni, a sociologist and professor at George Washington University, suggests that these two sources of individual motivation produce four forms of individual interaction with society.[12] We have represented these forms graphically in Figure 4. The four forms are involvements, duties, dictates, and asocial gratifications.

The diagram can be illustrated by reference to subjects with which we are all familiar—paying taxes and the 55-miles-per-hour speed limit law. Thirty years ago most Americans considered the payment of taxes a duty. While

Figure 4. How Individuals Interact with Society

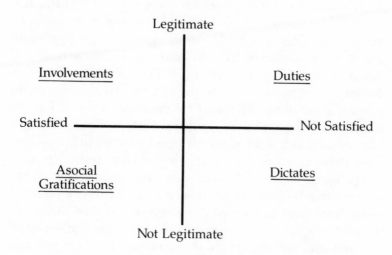

Legitimate

Involvements

Duties

Satisfied ———————————————— Not Satisfied

Asocial
Gratifications

Dictates

Not Legitimate

we can probably say with confidence that giving money to the government is seldom pleasurable and enjoyable, nevertheless most citizens felt it to be right, proper, and worthy of their support. Undoubtedly, paying taxes remains so for many; but it is also clear that a large group of Americans now pay their taxes, not out of duty and certainly not with a great deal of satisfaction, but as a dictate. To a great extent the behavior is now coerced under penalty of the law. One result is that tax cheating has greatly increased. The more a society must dictate behavior, the more controls must be initiated and the more people will tend toward quiet or overt rebellion.

Involvement and duty depend on mutual interdependence and agreement about what is right and proper. When mutual understanding in these matters decays and people pursue what is individually satisfying, then the isolation generates asocial gratification, which in turn spreads isolation. Many people seem to find driving 65 or 70 miles an hour satisfying, and they do so despite the laws to the contrary and the compelling evidence that 55 is safer for all. In spite of the bumpersticker message that "55 is a law we can live with," its legitimacy has never really been established. Etzioni calls behaviors that are not legitimate and that are based solely on individual satisfaction and pleasure "asocial gratifications." The word "asocial" is chosen carefully. It points to the reality that the pursuit of individual pleasure unfettered by the constraints of human interdependence makes no positive contribution to the ties that create and bond together a good community.

As these examples illustrate, legitimacy cannot be dictated. Social approval, a felt, seen, and experienced sense of understanding of our unity as human beings, a sense of partnership between people, is necessary before behaviors are acknowledged as legitimate. The narrower the bands of involvement, the smaller the segments of life where one can act on what one sees as proper, the more a situation is created that produces a sense of alienation from the world and the people in it. It is important to recognize that duty— behavior motivated by a sense of what is right—is closely related to the concept of loyalty. Fidelity, steadfastness, and trustworthy commitment are other words we use to describe the loyalty bonds that tie people together. "Loyalty commitments are like invisible but strong fibers which hold together complex pieces of relationship 'behavior' in families as well as in larger society. To understand the functions of a group of people, nothing is more crucial than to know who are bound together in loyalty and what loyalty means for them."[13]

Duties are the behavioral expressions of loyalty. They are the outward manifestations of people or groups keeping faith with one another and with the principles, values, norms, and symbols central to communal identity. Because there is finally no place to hide, duties and loyalties that exclude others and deny respect to them and to our fragile systems ultimately diminish all loyalty commitments. Few modern Americans need a lesson in the ways loyalty can be exploited, duty dishonored, and alienation increased when social consensus is lost as to the object of our duty.

It is well to remember that in human community what is done out of duty—that is, done for the mutual good—creates bonds of community, enhances the web of loyalty, and eventually brings the larger satisfaction of mutual contribution to the welfare of the whole. Our loss of social consensus on the objects of mutual good should not blind us to the fact that all behavior cannot be pleasurable or satisfying. It cannot be even when there is consensus. It can be a genuine nuisance to carry a sack full of trash in a crowded auto for several miles. Many acts required of family members are not very pleasurable in themselves. It is hard to feel jubilation at the prospect of scrubbing garbage cans. On the other hand, the continued mutual performance of even unpleasant duties leads over time to a bonding between people, to feelings of common concern and of shared experience that have a satisfaction all their own. Exercising initiative in the performance of public duties, those beyond the boundaries of our personal circle of loyalties, is an essential moral action for the restoration of the good-people system. Even the most ardent loyalty to our "own" group, church, or segment of society is not enough, because our created order insists on the mutuality of the whole human race.

When the marriage service says that this relationship is "for richer, for poorer—in sickness and in health" it reminds us that love only grows and endures when it is fed by both joy and duty. Duty and fidelity are not separable. As a sole source of motivation, personal gratification is a shallow well. With excessive use it is a well whose waters sour and contaminate the reciprocal ties of our moral ecology. The sudden loneliness and fear experienced on that beautiful Eastern shore road was a symptom of what happens when the actual experience of our interdependence with one another and with our world is broken.

Aldo Leopold, in talking of a land ethic, said that "a thing is right when it tends to preserve the integrity, stability and beauty of the biotic community. It is wrong when it tends otherwise."[14] There it is—a thing is right when it preserves our fragile interdependence and wrong when it does otherwise.

The shores of the Chesapeake Bay are littered with millions of varicolored and often intricately shaped plastic objects. A half-mile stroll down any beach will reveal hundreds of discarded containers, the arm of a doll, chunks of crumbling styrofoam, semideflated balls, long tangled lengths of plastic rope, the soles of shoes, and countless other relics of the invention of synthetic polymers. Unlike beach glass, which is rapidly changed by the action of wind and wave into the sand from which it came, the plastic remains. Over a period of years it will erode, but very gradually, worn away by the abrasion of the sand. But where do the abraded particles go? "The answer has just become apparent in a recent report. Nets that are used to collect microscopic organisms from the sea now accumulate a new material: tiny fragments of plastic fiber, often red, blue or orange."[15]

What are the connections, the interactions between crime on city streets, disease in an urban ghetto, child abuse in a family, apathy among the citizenry, and the plastic pollution of our world? Scientifically, we don't know and probably never will. Morally, we can be sure they are interdependent. Not just because they influence one another; "influence" is too weak a word to comprehend the systemic reality. The heart and lungs do not just influence one another. They are totally and completely interdependent parts of an integral whole that cannot be divided and live.

Our world is so complex and we have been so well schooled to separate, bifurcate, and isolate in order to understand how things work that from habit and a sense of isolation the impulse to take refuge with those who seem to be likeminded is almost irresistible. Like the invisible threads of plastic now a part of the oceans of the world, the moral consequences of our actions remain hidden and may never appear in our own lifetime. But those relics of our irresponsibility or loyalty are there. One need not stretch the imagination far to see that highway littering and human alienations are finally interrelated in a systemic whole. Wherever we live, whatever we do, each individual has the opportunity a thousand times a day to choose the right thing to preserve the oneness that is so often hidden to us.

ESCAPING THE TRAGEDY OF THE COMMONS

The tragedy of the commons is a now-famous metaphorical essay by the ecologist Garrett Hardin.[16] The commons Hardin refers to were the common pastures of colonial America and of the English village, which were open to all members of the community to graze their cattle. As the number of animals increased the supply of grass was insufficient. Hardin likens the ecosystem of the world to the common pasture, which presented a situation where the most sensible decision from an individual point of view is to increase the size of his or her own herd as rapidly as possible. One individual's unselfish behavior only leaves more grass for others and does nothing to prevent the eventual depletion of the pasture, so the sensible thing seems to be to graze while the grazing is good. Each person is locked into a process that moves slowly toward the inevitable ruin of the meadow and economic tragedy for all. The tragedy of the commons is a metaphor for those life situations in which the exercise of self-interest seems the only plausible course, because neither self-interest nor the refraining from it is able to stem the coming catastrophe. The history of water rights in our arid American West is a good example of a continuing struggle with the commons problem.

From the standpoint of public policy it is the dilemma of the "commons" problem that leads many people to turn to

government, and especially the federal government, to remedy the social ills. Whenever the boundaries of a systemic
problem are larger than the domain of the problem-solver,
often the only way to respond is to move to a higher level,
a broader authority. In Hardin's common pasture the problem was village-wide, but the only authority to deal with
it lay with the individual citizens.

In our everyday lives the moral equivalent of the common
pasture is the ecological and systemic pattern of our neighborhoods and small communities, whether they be small
towns or high-rise developments. Responsibility for the
overall health or goodness of the delicate network of place,
people, and living pattern that comprise the common moral
ground of our lives is divided up among many organizations with specialized responsibilities. There is a common
ground upon which all must feed in order to grow in the
knowledge of good and evil, but there is no agent or organization with responsibility for the health of the whole.

The lesson of the commons illustrates most clearly the
inadequacy of defining lay ministry, civic responsibility,
and social service within narrow institutional boundaries.
The commons metaphor should alert us that such narrow
definition is not only inadequate but also possibly destructive. What is in the self-interest of one institution may be
detrimental to the others.

A prevalent practice of American Protestantism has been
to establish congregations to serve local communities and
neighborhoods. Most of these congregations, however,
quickly take on the character of private membership associations as they compete head to head for the neighborhood
resources. To get the full implications of this, talk to any
new, young family in any neighborhood. As they contem-
plate the supports and resources they consider helpful in
building a strong marriage and family in that community,
the only way they can imagine receiving aid from a local
congregation is by joining and becoming active. They know

that the public school system and the public library offer their resources to all citizens. They assume, and probably rightly, that churches are set up to serve their own members, not the citizenry as a whole.

The competition between congregations for the most important resource of the neighborhood, its people, is certainly obvious. Most Americans assume that the private self-interest of the denominations is broadly in the interest of the general public. The broader issues of systems such as the commons do not come into consideration. Most Americans do not realize what a radical departure this is from much of the historical and cultural tradition of Christianity. In a way that is not comprehensible to modern Americans, historically the parish was the community.

The boundaries of the parish were the boundaries of the village, so that today, when the villages in their old form have disappeared, the parish boundaries are held to be good evidence of the former village boundaries. But common bounds were only the outward sign of something much more important which parish and village had in common: the congregation of the parish church was the body of all the villagers. The men who worked together worshipped together.[17]

This means that the everyday experience of the whole community was lived with a direct awareness of the moral connections between Christian precepts, parish worship, and the demands of the social situation. Public worship was truly public in that it existed for all. Thus it can truthfully be said that "the function of the mass in medieval society, like the great ceremonies of any society, was that of helping to maintain the sentiments on which the survival of the society depends.[18]

This possibility is precluded by the pluralistic and competitive situation of religion in American life. Urban American neighborhoods have become quite unstable in recent decades. Rapid change in the ethnic and socioeconomic profile of communities has become common. The cost and quality of the housing, the patterns of transportation, the availability of shops and stores, and the quality of the education available are just a few of the features of neighborhoods that have gone through rapid and turbulent transition. This has created a real problem for many local churches. Despite valiant struggles to recruit new members from populations very different from their own and to develop, with dwindling resources, programs of outreach to serve the community, many of these churches have been forced to close their doors and move to greener pastures, to neighborhoods where there are more families and more people who can be attracted to that particular denomination. Left behind, through no single institution's fault, is a neighborhood that is often bereft of resources and in which there is very little moral energy.

The Washington Post, in an article entitled "Lost in the City," described a Baltimore neighborhood in these words:

Outside the bars, there's not much to do in East Brooklyn. Encroaching industry has cut off most of the fishing and swimming once available along nearby Curtis Bay. St. Adalgert's Roman Catholic Church and a parish dance hall on Fourth Avenue burned down in the 1960s and were never rebuilt. Nowadays youths gather on the street corners, talking, drinking, smoking. The older folks sit on the front stoops of their homes.[19]

Service organizations, religious institutions, and volunteer associations—all the groups whose life and resources go together to make up a good community are trapped in such neighborhoods in the tragedy of the commons and have not known it. The harder each organization has worked to increase by drawing on the single resource base of the neighborhood, the more it has hoped to stay strong and be of service, but over the long haul it has contributed to the eventual decline of the neighborhood for all. The failure to see and regard the neighborhood as common property is obscured because the institutional herdspeople have been able to move on to new pastures and new forests when resources dwindled.

The metaphor of the commons should help us to see that our moral resources are not self-renewing unless careful conservation practices are supported by all. No single institution can act as if it had unlimited rights or responsibilities for the resources of family, friends, neighbors, and community networks. The preservation and health of this delicate ecology must be approached as a common problem or not approached at all. While it falls far short of being an adequate response to the commons issue, the place for individual citizens to begin is with a balanced appreciation for the diversity of associations and resources that must flourish for there to be health. Casting one's whole lot with even the most benevolent herdsperson will not solve the problem of the common moral ground from which all must obtain food, or none will be nourished.

This is not a happy message for the man or woman who is pouring energy into the renewal of a particular local group or church in an effort to preserve the best qualities of life in that community. But it offers a starting point. A group of friends recently found themselves redistricted into a different elementary school district whose reputation and network of educational resources were considerably below the district they had been in. One of the parents involved commented, "I guess we now have to work as hard on that school district as we have on the one we just left—it is all the same system and we know a lot more, so maybe we can do some good." The reality is that all must grow, all must share in the costs and benefits of our common ground for any of us to have long-term health.

NO ONE KNOWS

Extremely complex systems, and that is what we are talking about, are hard to understand and predict. They often appear simple on the surface. As a result good intentions, simple and obvious solutions, are often foolishly wrong. Sometimes the true moral consequences of our decisions will not be known for generations. It has taken hundreds of years to come to the recognition that to be our neighbor's keeper is more than a nice moral precept. The fact that it is an exacting and irrevocable law of the created order is hidden because the actual outcome and results are often far removed from our initial action.

Villagers in a section of Africa were troubled by hippopotamuses coming up from the river to graze in the village gardens. A successful campaign was undertaken to kill off the hippos. But in the ensuing months many of the villagers became ill with a strange new disease. It took some time to discover the cause and to uncover the systemic connection between the eradication of the hippos and the illness of the villagers. "The disease was caused by an organism which had bred in the mud along the river. When the hippopotamuses churned up the mud they killed most of the eggs and kept the organism under control."[20]

Complex systems fool us because the relation of cause to effect is not immediately visible. Often well-intended actions lead to distant, unexplained, and often negative consequences. Liberals and conservatives alike are beginning to recognize that many of our public welfare programs, planned with the best motives, have had unwholesome consequences for the moral health of our society.

Peter Senge, a faculty member of the MIT Sloan School of Management, teaches an excellent seminar on leadership in complex systems. Most attendees are experienced upper-level executives in high-tech organizations and their spouses. When we attended this seminar, at one point everyone was invited to participate in diagramming the systemic functioning of a small, fast-growing, start-up company. Senge and his colleagues covered one whole wall of the conference room with blank white paper. For an hour the conferees directed the staff in filling the paper with lines, arrows, and captions, charts of the multiple pathways of interaction and influence among the expanding list of organizational elements and forces. Many participants had actually been part of similar situations and so were able to clarify and add depth to the discussion.

Finally Senge stopped the action. By now the entire wall was covered with an incredible profusion of symbols and labels. Senge asked the group who really understood how this system functioned. After a long silence, someone stammered out, "No one." After this participants debated whether or not in some distant future there will be a computer program that can comprehend the working of such a system. Reluctantly, everyone agreed with the point Senge spent so much time helping us to understand: No one knows and no one will ever know the intricate interdependencies of even this small organization.

It is a hard lesson. But that sample organizational system is infinitely less complex than the moral ecology out of which the pattern and story of our lives is woven. The fact that we can never really know the moral consequences of our actions does not mean that those actions are free from the authority of eternal and unchanging laws. Nor does it mean that we have any excuse for not acting with as much wisdom as we can muster. It does mean that there is a need to value and develop a style of learning that has room for the language of the heart as well as the language of science.

The economist and futurist Robert Theobald believes that new patterns of teaching and learning will emerge as more and more people recognize the fact of interconnection and interdependence. "The need is for an overall perspective which will provide a basis for decision making. Those who try to develop overall understandings are still scarce in our culture and typically even less available in academic circles which are organized to perpetuate the disciplines."[21]

This kind of perspective can only be gained by actively

engaging those who are involved in working for a better society. Wendell Berry is one such person. His writings reflect the wisdom of someone who can allow understanding to grow from a gentle and persistent care for our mutual interdependence. Listen to his understanding of the way our complex systems deceive us in the formulation of everyday life.

If I step off the roof I will fall immediately; if in this age of nuclear weapons, toxic chemicals, rampant disruption of soil, etc., we do not love one another, we or our children will suffer for it sometime. It is a critical difference, for it explains why people who do not ever willingly step off a roof will fearlessly regard their neighbors as enemies or competitors or economic victims. The uncertainty of the term between offense and punishment licenses all our viciousness, foolishness and pride.[22]

Systems theory has sometimes been called the dismal science because of the cold water it pours on the ability of science to build a better world. Berry writes not as a scientist but as a farmer and a poet. He tells of the Old Order Amish, who, using traditional methods, have in the last thirty years remained in farming and have doubled their population. In this same period thousands of mechanized farmers have quit or gone broke and have left the land. Berry believes that the reasons for this defy analysis because they involve an order of magnitude and complexity that is beyond comprehension. "The real or whole reason must be impossibly complicated, having to do with nature, culture, religion, family and community life, as well as with agricultural methodology and economics."[23]

Our experience is that after some initial hesitation, based on a fear that others may sit in judgment, people generally are starved for vocabulary and learning to help them put their daily experience into a complete moral perspective. The fact that no one can tell us precisely what brings harmony and good into a situation is in truth a summons to freedom *and* responsibility.

BUILDING AND RESTORING WHOLENESS

A major emphasis of systems theory is on connectedness, on what holds a system together so that it functions effectively and in harmony with itself. Too many individuals and groups in American life feel a sense of distance from significant participation in the building of a just and good society, and this is a direct consequence of the fragmentation of the moral order.

An effective good-people system is based on a felt sense of interdependence with other people and with the natural order. To realize such wholeness we will need to change our ways of thinking, enrich our vocabularies, add to the opportunities for public service, and strengthen the total fabric of the local communities, which are the basic building blocks of a good society. Our present thinking, vocabulary, forms of public service, and experiences of community all too often simply continue, extend, and deepen the fragmentation that is so inimical to the moral order. The individual, the family, the neighborhood, and all those institutions that go into creating and sustaining the fabric of a neighborhood comprise a single system—an undivided whole—the good-people system. But our thinking, our vocabulary, and most of our institutional practices lead us to see, not the whole system, but separate, unrelated parts.

Our approach is too fragmentary and its illusory perceptions and categories of thought and language continue to confuse and distort.

Even our ways of regarding the elements of the crucial good-people system serve to increase division. When we think of a person, we talk and act as if the psyche and the soma were separate parts of the individual. When we think of families, we picture married people with 2.5 children. When we think of neighborhoods, we envision rows of houses. Many of these divisions are false and contribute to the disarray and evil in the world. Thus, while it seems that the world is rife with "we-they" and "win-lose" situations, the reality is that every "they" and "we" are one and the same.

In his book *Wholeness and the Implicate Order*, David Bohm, a theoretical physicist, explores many of the implications of our fragmentary views of the cosmos. He points to the central fallacy of assuming that any of the ways we think about the world represent the way it really is. There is a oneness, he suggests, between the content of thought and the process that produces that thinking, so that "the illusion that the self and the world are broken into fragments originates in the kind of thought that goes beyond its proper measure and confuses its own product with the same independent reality."[24]

For the most part our institutional experience takes place within large, professionalized bureaucracies with specialized vocabularies and specialized forms of service and work. This makes it difficult to find the words to live by and to stand by. Few of our words seem to speak of deeds for the public good. People who share common experiences also share common words, a common vocabulary. A strong, cohesive moral fabric means we share words that refer directly to communal experience. A whole community will have stories and shared experiences that maintain their direct link with the words of vital moral discourse.

What makes a system a whole is the marvelously intricate interdependencies between the embedded elements of the system. Speaking as a farmer, Wendell Berry describes the fragmentation that occurs when one begins to talk of the industrialization of milk production and to speak of a cow as a manufacturing unit. In this situation the moral connection between a family and a cow breaks down. This connection was at one time real enough to be expressed as "be good to the cow for she is our companion."[25]

The multiplicity of connections between an individual, a

family, a neighborhood, and all those institutions that go into making a neighborhood can be shattered, and in many cases already have been. Because we still see farmers and cows and can buy milk, we don't recognize that anything has been broken, that vital linkages have been destroyed. Because we still see people and homes with parents and children and churches on the corner and schools in the neighborhood, we don't realize that critical connections have been broken. These connections do not occur naturally, they are formed through effort, propriety, discipline, and duty. Through the dynamics of companionship a moral bond is forged between a family and its cow. This interdependency is experienced as a duty and is upheld by simple shared words born of the common experience. The connections of a family within itself and with its neighborhood require the same discipline.

To restore and build wholeness is the central moral task of our society. It is a task that must be done by the layperson. It can be done best by those in situations where there is a common status as neighbors, citizens, seekers, and servants of a decent, just, and good world. We shall try to determine what care and service mean in the general building and repair of the good-people system.

3. The Family and Good People

"What is it that causes so many people to lead such barren lives?" asked a friend who is a dedicated, intelligent therapist and family researcher. His question is important. A moral life will not be barren. It may be sad, it may be poor, it may have great periods of sorrow and tragedy, but it will not be barren, sterile, or unfruitful. A life can be affluent, marked by privilege and power, and still be desolate and morally unproductive. Many apparently prosperous lives are empty enough to generate this friend's searching question.

The Bible tells us that "the fruit of the righteous is a tree of life" (Prov. 11:30); but in the dazzling array of our supermarket culture there is no effective consumer guidance for finding this particular fruit. Part of the difficulty is the variety of substitutes and alternatives available. Barren lives can be filled with an endless array of activities—so can fruitful lives. When our political parties urge civic responsibility and active participation in a democratic society; when religious groups urge commitment to social ministry and outreach; when public service agencies ask for dollars and volunteer energy; all are trying to operate and provide guidance in the face of the same problem—a society that has trouble being fruitful because too many of its members are leading barren lives.

Central to this problem is the need for moral literacy and self-determination. People need to know that they are a part of a story that makes a difference—a story that is fertile with meaning. They need to understand through experience that they can be active authors and agents in the creation of this story. A productive life of moral literacy and self-determination would manifest certain characteristics:

- a reflective and personal relation to the active, working story of a people and of a community where there is a continuity and purpose
- a personal vision, a potentially realizable future state rich with values and meaning and which manifests an interdependence and interconnection with the past and with other people
- the initiative and courage to act on the vision, to make daily decisions that serve and promote the desired future

One must begin with one's own community—the place where he or she is a part of the story. In most cases this is the family, the situation in which one first begins to know the story. For this reason the family is very important to the good-people system. Unfortunately, of all the arenas for moral expression in our society, none is more filled with confusion and false possibility than the family. It is a hot spot representing the primary situation in which the moral life is nurtured, and yet in today's society the situation is one of moral confusion.

A key staff member in a national agency of a major Protestant denomination recalls his efforts to develop a program strategy that would plainly state the normal value of marriage and child-rearing. "What I wanted to do wasn't to return to some mythical past, but to take a clear stance on the importance of a stable family and try to have that vision take into account the many issues of two-career marriages." His effort was met by hostility and outrage that he would raise the subject and by implication demean divorced, single, and gay people. The discussion was short and charged with emotion. Genuine exploration of the question was neither possible nor desired by most of the group. His initiative had been based on the belief that the church has an obligation to set standards and give support to fruitful visions. The group's rejection was based on a belief that such a standard would trample on the rights and freedoms of those who by choice or life circumstance were in a different place.

"Have we done the right thing in having a baby?" This question can be asked as a complaint stemming from a selfish and self-centered desire for personal liberty to do as one pleases. But it can also be a deeply moral question asked by a sincere searcher for truth in a society where the moral worth of the family is being seriously challenged. Susan is a dedicated and competent social worker whose husband is a social service doctor. Both of them see their careers as direct expressions of their deeply held humanistic values. Now Susan's career has been interrupted by the birth of their first child, and she asks, "Have we done the right thing in having a baby?" not because she is selfish and self-indulgent, but because she and her husband are discovering first-hand the demands a baby makes on time, physical energy, and emotional endurance. They are working together to share the chores and to balance the commitments necessary to make their home and family system work. They had planned this pregnancy deliberately and looked forward to the coming of their child with joy. Now their energies, formerly devoted fully to working and struggling with and for others, are being diverted and sorely tested by a small, helpless, demanding infant who is going to be with them for a long time. In today's world one can understand Susan's question.

One major reason for our present confusion is that for possibly the first time in history we have a society that regards the individual rather than the family as the fundamental unit, the basic building block, of civilization. "The high divorce rate, the large number of single-parent families, and the public's willingness to work toward a more egalitarian society through interventions that abrogate the family's power make the person the central entity in the eyes of the law, the school, and the self,"[1] says Jerome Kagan, professor of developmental psychology at Harvard University. He also reports some revealing comments by a young divorced woman with a small child who states that she cannot be dependent on anyone, that she must develop herself. Kagan believes that this deep-seated attitude begins with the one-sided emphasis Americans place on children being autonomous people, independent of their parents. "For many middle-class families, the child is a beautiful young bird to be cared for until it is ready to fly free in the forest."[2]

A very close friend was responsible in large measure for the founding of an extremely creative and innovative preschool. Central to the genius of the school was its interaction with the total family. Through the cooperative involvement of the parents and through an integral program of home teaching, the school achieved growth for children, parents, and the family as a system. After some years away from the school my friend returned recently to consult with the present faculty and staff. While she found the school healthy and thriving with its range of programs still essentially intact, one of her findings was not so salutary. "I was surprised," she said, "to find that the staff spoke only of their educational goals for the individual child and that the value and philosophy of the original emphasis upon the family was no longer a part of the school's promotional literature or the focused attention of the staff. This shift had not gone unnoticed and was intentional. It was made, I believe, because we live in a society whose normal and natural emphasis is upon the individual rather than the family unit."

Even the meaning of the term "family" is a matter of confusion and a further reflection of the perplexed state of affairs. There are at least three positions in the contemporary controversy over the use and meaning of the word "family." One position has to do with politics and power.

The traditional American middle-class definition of family as husband, wife, and two or three children is a political target for many groups fighting for legitimacy and power in American society. Thus many homosexual couples and individuals have sought a definition of "families" that is pluralistic and includes a wide variety of relationships. To talk of "families" rather than "family" is the goal, since it suggests a variety of structures and arrangements that can be labeled a family. A second perspective on the definition is influenced by demographic factors and a desire to be adequately descriptive. Here the advocate is dealing with such factors as the enormous number of single-parent homes and the issue is the adequacy of a definition that excludes more situations than it includes. The third perspective is an attempt to be normative—when we say "family," what is the valued vision that we intend to describe? Unfortunately, most debates, formal or informal, have only served to blur these distinctions. There is a widespread tendency in American society to let demographic data determine legitimacy. Part of this may be due to the degree that political ends are served by blurring the distinction between the ideals we value and the variations and deviations that our pollsters count and measure.

The definition we will work with here is avowedly normative. It is the understanding of the family that we wish to advocate, defend, and preserve. At the same time we believe it is a definition that makes sense even to many Americans who are not living within a household comprised of a wife, husband, and children. The ideal, practical pattern for the family should include at least three generations of blood kin, and that family net should spread out to include those other neighbors, associates, and families tied by involvement and friendship into an actual working partnership with the focal family unit. This systemic or holistic definition of the family is what people must learn to value and strive to emulate. One subsystem of this total family is the intact, traditional nuclear family. But a whole family includes not only mom and dad and sons and daughters. It includes granddad and grandmother, Uncle Joe, Cousin Ruth who is single, and it includes those individuals and family systems who have intimate, dependable, regular interaction with the core family unit. A colleague, for example, takes great pleasure in reporting that his own family is unanimous, explicit, and clear in counting two other nuclear families with whom they have no blood ties as fundamental parts of their own. In times of crisis and in times of joy outsiders would be hard pressed to know who is related and who is not. Their lives are harmoniously enmeshed. There is a regularity of communication, a sharing of rituals and celebrations, a mutual history of story and event, an understanding of confidentiality and support within that total family that differs from outsiders and that extends to such legal arrangements as wills and partnerships. There is a special sense of solidarity that binds them all together. In such a situation one would not think of saying there is no one to depend on but oneself.

Every citizen, young or old, single, divorced, married, remarried, has the opportunity, and even the obligation, to be a part of a total family system. Each traditional nuclear family has the possibility of becoming the anchor unit for a total family. Society does not provide these possibilities cheaply; a vibrant total family is the result of intention and work.

A single individual cannot create or maintain a true marriage or a family system. Some people choose, perhaps wisely, or are shaped by life circumstances never to marry or never to have children. These persons can and should be active, responsible members of a total family. For their own sake and for the common good, each nuclear family needs to move outside the warm shelter of domesticity to take part in the building of a total family. This definition of the total family excuses no one from the active support and advocacy of the family system as the indispensable and primary unit of a free, just, and moral society.

There are, of course, many possible limitations on significant choice and intentional deliberative action in all our lives. For every person the accidents of genetic heritage, the restrictions of environment, ethnic background, social status, and economic position shape to a large degree who we are, what we become, where we live, what we do, and who our friends are. Everyday life, which is the primary reality for each of us, seems after only a few years to be filled with obligations, requirements, and commitments that fall into one's lap with remorseless regularity and repetition. How many choices do we get to make that will really shape the character of our story? How many actions are we given that have the potential to shape history—to leave the world different than we found it? Susan felt she had played one of the big cards in the game of life in the decision to bear a child, and she was right. So many barren lives consist of sterile activity without vision or value. Seen up close the life of a Palm Beach millionaire, enjoying sport fishing, luxury automobiles, masseuses, European travel, formal dinner parties, investment planning, can be as devoid of fruitful moral yield as that of a reclusive, isolated, poor and miserly addict to the afternoon soaps.

Walker Percy's novels attempt in an indirect way to answer Susan's question. His stories are about a world filled with multiple, misleading conventions as to what life is all about. His heroes and heroines are fallible, half-crazy, self-doubting searchers beset by temptation, tribulation, and human frailty as they stumble through life. They are not mighty, but they are real and they are good. Not good in the limited sense of prim, proper, and convention bound, but good because part of their craziness is their restiveness with moral illiteracy and their crablike movement and courageous forays to discover what is fruitful and right. His searchers are people like Fran making her list of priorities and Susan with her troubled question, both fumbling for discoveries that bring forth the fruit of a rich life. The search often leads to discovery of the enduring context of the family. "To bed we go for a long winters' nap," says Percy at the end of *Love in the Ruins*, "twined about each other as the ivy twineth, not under a bush or in a car or on the floor or any such humbug as marked the past peculiar years of Christendom, but at home in bed where all good folk belong."[3]

The poet Margaret Atwood penned a caustic line, "[The] civilized world is a zoo, not a jungle, stay in your cage."[4] For many people the family has been perceived as a cage with confining bars and restrictive security. A middle-aged male acquaintance recently gave a young man this common advice, "Wait a while to get married—don't lose your freedom yet." How sad! Marriage is not a prison. In marriage good people can be alive, vital, engaged. Courage, exploration, action, love, advocacy, service, loyalty are some of the qualities that make the lives of good people fruitful rather than barren, dull, or boring. The family is, despite the humbug of recent years, the place of the heart—not the heart of weak sentiment, worn out rules, and pale piety, but of abundant courage, wisdom, passion, and understanding from which flow the springs of life (Prov. 4:23).

THE MORAL SIGNIFICANCE OF THE TOTAL FAMILY

Good and whole families are created, not found ready-made; but they are not monuments built only to be preserved and admired. The well-made family, the one developed thoughtfully and with care, provides a network for love, for discovery, for responding to grief, for forgiveness, for mutual interaction, and for reaching out to others. There are many reasons why the family is the keystone of the good-people system: Our most innate and personal sense of both care and justice are essentially shaped within the cradle of the family. At all ages and stages of life we choose the primary group relationships that do so much to shape our moral worldview through the family. The family system serves as the base of operations for the great bulk of our moral contribution to society.

THE FAMILY AS THE CRADLE OF CARE AND JUSTICE

It is absolutely certain that schools, churches, synagogues, child-care centers, youth associations, and all the other institutions we rely on in the formidable task of bringing up our children will fail if the family fails. Urie Bronfenbrenner, professor of human development and family studies at Cornell University, states that in "recent years nearly every line of social and psychological research points to the family as the foremost influence in what the Germans call 'erziehung,' the Russians 'vospitanie,' the French 'elevation,' the Greeks 'paideia,' and we might call 'character formation,' 'cultural education' or 'upbringing'."[5]

Peter and Brigette Berger, writing as sociologists and social critics, express it simply: "The family, today as always, remains the institution in which at any rate the very great majority of individuals learn whatever they will ever learn about morality."[6] But the fact is that while this reality has been rather widely adopted as a slogan, its implications for the way we run our institutions and shape our lives remain largely unrealized. It is time to look more closely at what it means to say that the family is the cradle of care and justice.

Carol Gilligan is a social scientist who has done research on a theory she calls a "morality of care." Her work is a convincing argument that moral truth is exceedingly complex and that present theories of moral development as exemplified by Kohlberg and Piaget are built on narrowly masculine, overly rational concepts of justice, rights, and rules to the neglect of a more feminine ethic of care and responsibility. The justice ethic uses a vocabulary that is analytical and preoccupied with equality, fairness, balance, and reciprocity. The ethic of care has a vocabulary that expresses love, care, friendship, and hurt. Justice grows in the first ethic with educated, thoughtful participation in our democratic social institutions. Care is fostered through an understanding of our wholeness and interdependence. Thus the emphasis in the second ethic is upon those experiences that over time reveal our connectedness and the consequences of our actions upon others. "The age-old dialogue between justice and love, reason and compassion, fairness and forgiveness, reflects not just two opposing or complementary conceptions of the moral domain but the fundamental tension in human psychology between the experience of separation and the experience of connection."[7]

The cradle for both justice and care, for the experience of separation and connection, is the family. Gilligan reports a pivotal moral experience of a thirty-year-old female research subject. This woman had a dream when her baby was very small. In the dream their home catches fire, and so vivid was the dream that the woman awoke in an anxious panic over the safety of her child. This experience brought the young mother to the certain realization that if the dream had been real she would have tried to save the baby at all costs. "Lying there in the dark, I realized that there was an absolute in my life, this unquestionable absolute in my life, and it made me feel very relaxed, and I remember feeling very calm; why yes there is something I would put far, far higher than anything to do with myself. . . ."[8] Such precious insight is hard to come by outside the family. An ethic of care depends upon a morality of love, of the knowledge and experience in a relationship that is responsive to the care and wants of others. The first realization most of us can have that there is no greater love than giving up your life to save another comes as it did to this young woman in the relationship of parent and child.

Some family-system therapists see a similar and equally vital connection to the ethic of justice in the dynamics of family life. Justice, fairness, equity, duty, and loyalty are regarded as the major forces governing the transactions between family members. Families are bound together by an unconscious ledger of merit that each member continually addresses and balances by acts of obligation, exploitation, and rights assertions.

Whereas the ideal goal of judicial systems consists in an approximation of a just society, based on essentially shared principles of equity, the justice of everyday human interactions is continually being assessed in the minds and hearts of the persons involved. Exploitation of a material kind can be quantified, but personal exploitation is measurable only on a subjective scale which has been built into the person's sense of the meaning of his entire existence.[9]

Children are often quick to point out that a brother or sister is "getting away with murder." If this sense of injustice continues unattended, without instruction or redress, it can fester and spread to the wider society. The result is damage to one's basic trust in our interdependence, our common obligation to one another. Justice demands some accounting, a balancing of the ledger, if a sense of a just society is to be preserved.

At the moment of birth the parents "owe" the child a debt of care and responsibility. From this starting point each of us shares in the exchange of virtues and vices as parent and child work out their experiential answers to such questions as, "What does each child deserve?" "How much gratitude do I owe to my parents?" "What rights do each of us have as members of this family?" "What do we do when the ledger gets out of balance?" Unsettled accounts are passed on from generation to generation: "I'll give my child what I never got." "I learned from my father that men can never be trusted."

In a recent movie a teenage boy is shot by the police—shot because he is holding a gun and is too frightened and confused to surrender quickly. The scene seemed overdrawn, distracting, and artificial to a friend who went to see the film. The real excitement was provided by a young man sitting three rows down who suddenly exclaimed, "Those pigs, just because they have guns they think they can get away with murder!" His sudden real-life identification with the scene was a sharp jolt. One wonders what experiences of justice and injustice had caused such a reaction to this scene that had little dramatic impact for most viewers.

There are no judges, juries, lawyers, or legal codes to adjudicate, regularize, and rationalize issues of justice within the family. Family justice involves the intersubjective judgments of the family members. The ability to discriminate in matters of justice and injustice is first formed in the emotional dynamic of reciprocal family relationships. This training is important, not only to the development of the individual, but to the development of a society whose citizens can take an active and measured role in the establishment of justice.

All the researchers, therapists, and cadres of professionals who have made the family their topic have not come up with many clear rules and guidelines for family living. The wide variety of domestic, marital, and family relationships prevailing today creates a confused picture from which to infer values, ideals, and vision with regard to this most important and most traditional site of character formation. But even in this confusion it remains clear that the central importance of family life is the formation of good people. Brigette Berger says, "All the evidence we have available to us unambiguously indicates that the single most powerful harm that comes to children is derived from the lack of family or family-like structures and arrangements."[10] If it is true that the good-people system works like compound interest and goodness begets goodness, then to disrupt the system is to put our society in serious trouble. Healthy family systems are central to the well-being of the good-people system and hence to the welfare of the world.

THE IMPORTANCE OF OUR FRIENDS

We all know the world is round. We learned it in school, and we have seen the pictures from space. Most of the time we do not have to think about it or change our behavior to adjust to that reality. We can act as if the world were flat.

Most of us are aware that our character and our choices about what is right and proper are heavily influenced by our friends. We learned in school or from the media about the importance of reference groups, of significant others, of our network of social support in shaping our values, forming our behavioral patterns, and transmitting moral concepts. Numerous social-psychology studies show that the more an individual is reminded of his or her member-ship in a significant social group, the more that person reflects the values, ideals, and norms of that group. This is a reality we take for granted. What a difference there could be if we made the conscious effort to see ourselves and our families as linked together and to friends and friend-families in a web of fragile but powerful filaments through which our dearest values and ideas pulse as through a network of veins and arteries. From this perspective any consideration of oneself or one's immediate family would encompass a much wider set of individuals and families. The ties that bind us to one another are as real as the ties that bind and integrate the self. Where does the self begin and end? Where does the family begin and end?

Raoul Naroll, a social anthropologist, has coined the term "moralnets" to describe the social network of friends, friend-families, and significant others who do so much to shape one's moral choices. Naroll has written an entire book detailing his conclusion, based on studies the world over, that societies where crime, alcoholism, delinquency, mental illness, and other kinds of abuse are low have strong, well-integrated moralnets. He finds the research evidence overwhelming that weakened moralnets lead to human suffering and to increased susceptibility to both physical and mental illness. As moralnets weaken, the prevalence of these social and physical ills increases. The family is the most common and most central means through which people are tied significantly to a moralnet, and hence it is the key to the moral order of our society. Naroll repeatedly cites research indicating that families that are successful, as judged by the mental and social health of their children, are families that have strong ties, important linkages with at least five other families. It is as if our moral order is dependent on a specific social ecology that may seem elusive and yet is easy to find if we know where to look.[11]

This may mean that the most important thing one can do to remedy the wide range of social ills that plague our culture—child abuse, suicide, spouse abuse, alcoholism, mental illness, and so on—is to work to become a part of a whole family system and then see to it that the family develops a substantive relationship with five other families. Here is an action within the reach of every single man and woman, which could perhaps do more good than all of the social service programs could ever hope to accomplish. Instead of creating more programs to make the world more loving and just, it is urgent to move on what is in the reach of each of us, the strengthening and enriching of our moralnets.

William Phipps, professor of religion and philosophy at Davis and Elkins College, has pointed out that

the life of the earliest Christian community, in Jerusalem, may afford a clue to this more inclusive life. These Christians were able, at least temporarily, to expand the communal bond of ideal family life by sharing their possessions. Transcending a mine-thine dichotomy, they received from members according to their abilities and gave to them according to their needs.[12]

Recently, the chief officers of a small business firm were describing the personal and family difficulties of one of their key employees. Included in the list were suspected child abuse, desertion, and mental illness. Despite their efforts to lend support, the employee's problems were overwhelming his capacity to work effectively. The two officers had very reluctantly informed the man that unless something changed they would be forced to remove him from his job. One of the executives remarked, "What this fellow needs is a family to lean on." Though the lack of a significant social support, or a moralnet, is often hidden to the individuals involved, it is the most common ingredient in troubled lives. A family might think that it has loads of friends, when in reality the adults have a great many social or business acquaintances and cocktail party companions, and the children and teenagers have their own circle of companions. A young girl confided one day that she had come to realize her parents didn't have any real friends, and as a result her family was not genuinely in relationship with any other family. Unfortunately, this truth was hidden from her mother and father.

Every individual can join and participate in a whole family, and every such family can work to create a moralnet of three to five other friend-families. Admittedly, what one would be intentionally creating are structures and relationships that in a healthy society occur naturally and without conscious effort. But our society is deeply troubled and filled with forces that tear at the natural supports. In such a situation some guidelines to help create a strong family moralnet are in order. For some families such guided effort will lead only a few steps beyond what they have already naturally created. For other families, if they are able to recognize themselves, these guidelines can represent a major change in style of living.

1. *Acknowledge the relationship.* Friend-families need to know that they are intentional friends. It may seem awkward and embarrassing to state clearly your desire for such

a relationship when the usual social custom is to assume friendship only after the "proper" amount of time and interaction have occurred. But the relationship should not be assumed; it will grow and mature if jointly and openly acknowledged. This will allow each family to share in shaping the relationship and in assuming responsibility for keeping it healthy.

2. *Create shared rituals.* Whether it be holiday festivals, birthday celebrations, or invented occasions, shared rituals are fundamental to friend-family relationships. These times generate the stories and treasured memories that embed the affiliation in the heart, and provide enduring vitality.

Several friend-families in one solid and vibrant moralnet gather for an annual Easter service on the beach. Children decorate the table with treasures gleaned from both meadow and shore. Stories and significant moments from the past year are told. Bread and wine are shared. It has become the annual event, a time when they honor and give thanks for the bonds that hold them together.

3. *Develop the trust to share problems.* Families develop secrets, and secrets accrue the power to distort emotion, reason, and memory. Being able to submit the multiple problems and demands of family life to a reality test is one of the great benefits of a moralnet. There are no real experts to consult before responding to the ordinary dilemmas of family life. The perspective of other reliable human beings and the chance to talk through one's own perspective can inform and empower responsible action.

Defensiveness, arrogance, betrayal through gossip, and an inability to listen will, of course, undermine the trust that is necessary. The least obvious but best remedy for these trust-destroying vices is open, firm, and compassionate exposure as soon as one appears.

4. *Spend enough time together.* People often talk about special friends they have not seen for years, but with whom they know they could pick right up as if there had been no separation. Undoubtedly, many have had this experience of

instant renewal. Nevertheless, the importance of a moralnet rests in great measure on the constancy of interaction. The social supports of mutual obligation, personal affirmation, and the regular voluntary exchange of values and information depend on a constancy and immediacy of interaction. Two key friend-families in one moralnet live some two thousand miles apart, and have been separated by this distance for most of the twenty years of their relationship. Both families have worked and planned so that they are together at least twice a year. Monthly phone calls and lengthy letters help to fill in the gaps. Maintaining these ties has cost money and considerable thought and attention. But they feel the friendship is worth the price.

Good intentions are no substitute for specific plans that create time together. Agreements to share an annual camping trip, or the ritual of opening day at the ballpark, or sharing in a neighborhood food coop, are decisions that move beyond good intentions to create a structure that ensures the opportunity to be together.

5. *Consciously balance diverse and common attributes.* Think for a moment about the way a moralnet functions to provide a setting in which children can experience a different way of perceiving the world and acting in it, one that is different from the patterns of their own immediate family. Moralnets broaden horizons within a climate that securely encourages exploration. At the same time the moralnet is a powerful means of reinforcing key values and their attendant styles of living. Other significant adults may become mentors and role models for the developing child, providing clear and ready examples to emulate. A moralnet is not a group. It is unlikely that any one individual or any one family in a moralnet will select the same set of persons, the same network configuration as any other individual or family. Overlap may be quite considerable, but the freedom exists to create one's own network and set of linkages. Functioning as a network rather than a group, a moralnet can accommodate diversity beyond the limits of most groups.

Accordingly, a moralnet should form on the basis of shared values but should encompass as much diversity as possible. Age diversity, for instance, allows for the wisdom of veterans and the freshness of new generations. A moralnet may be one of the few places in society where religious diversity can be explored and experienced at a personal and intimate level. One of the great hazards of American life is that most of one's friends can be, and indeed often are, found within the bounds of one's profession or the confines of one's corporate or institutional allegiance. Not unexpectedly, one result is that the whole world begins to be viewed through the lens of the corporate culture of that institution. To grow a healthy and vital pluralistic society, it is critical that we grow moralnets that move beyond such parochial boundaries.

One can and should create guidelines out of the experience of one's own family system, but the five guides offered here should prove helpful. The important thing is that every individual and every family has the opportunity to make a substantive contribution to a better world through the family system and the moralnets they can create and sustain.

THE FAMILY AS CREATIVE CENTER

For the good-people system to place so much confidence in the family and neighborhood seems to some to ignore the power and influence on our world and society of such mega-institutions as the multinational corporation or the modern nation-state. The massive evidence that the moralnet, with the family system at its heart, is crucial to a healthy society is not enough to get the attention of those who are counting on scientifically engineered solutions and the might of large-scale programs to shape our world. What is required is a change in focus, a new vision of the power of the individual citizen to make a lasting contribution to our world.

A father and mother turned to their pastor for help in

dealing with their troubled and rebellious daughter. The couple described their frustration because they were receiving such conflicting signals from different members of the helping professions. A succession of five separate therapists, counselors, and doctors had been approached for help and advice. To the couple's ears each expert seemed to suggest a different answer and approach to their problem. As the pastor listened he realized they were seeking a formula they could follow to resolve their difficulties. The pastor tried gently to help the couple see that their search was in vain. No one can provide an engineering blueprint for the construction of family life. By focusing their attention on this vain search and on the inadequacy of the helpers the couple was in effect rejecting all help and avoiding their responsibility for their own actions.

This story is an illustration of the power of what we attend to. The objects of our attention, the focus of our concentration, the themes of our vision are choices we all make, and they are dramatic indications of what we really care about. Moreover, as stated so clearly by a Christian educator, Craig Dykstra, the qualitative character of the individual is in turn shaped by the character or quality of that attention. "Acts of attention do not leave us unchanged. Each new act of attention broadens not only our world, but also our capacity to see deeply into that world. When other people or things or ideas are received by us through our realistic perception of them, we are not left as we were."[13]

As we have frequently noted, our culture continually focuses our attention on organizational and engineering solutions to the complexities of life in modern society. Too many people are convinced that only the expert can speak in an informed manner. Our culture has lost touch with the subtle, powerful, mysterious ties that bind our lives together.

A young man recently enrolled in a masters program

largely populated by professional engineers. One course had been on human behavior in organizations. He was describing the difficulty some of his fellow students were having because the instructor would never provide a blueprint, only principles and guidelines to be applied situationally. He explained, "As a physics major I find that easier to accept than the engineers. I know that uncertainty is fundamental to the nature of the universe." Our culture still drinks deeply at the trough of the unwarranted confidence that we can know all there is to know and technologically create whatever we put our minds to. We are still like the oft-cited *New Yorker* cartoon in which the man loudly proclaims that *he can too* put Humpty Dumpty back together again if we will only provide more horses and more king's men.

The entirely different perspective of such countercultural people as Aldo Leopold or Wendell Berry is one of attention to the multiplicity of connections and the bonds of care and love that tie people to people and people to a home or a plot of ground. Interdependencies of familiarity, commitment, memory, propriety, restraint, and care are the bonds upon which they urge us to focus with disciplined attention. And nowhere is there more necessity and possibility for such attention than in the mysterious and infinite interdependencies of the family system and its moralnet. This possibility is open to each one of us and with equal opportunity for all. Those who do live in such interdependencies have vitality and life, almost without regard to other circumstance.

Elise Boulding, social researcher and professor at Dartmouth College, has studied the genesis of community resources in the early stages of new town development. Should it surprise us to learn that the family is the wellspring of initiative from which the significant social institutions in the community flow? Is it a surprise that involvement in the family generates the motivation to make this a good place for children to grow up and live?[14]

The surprise is that we must be told of the social inventiveness of the family and reminded that the usual focus of our attention in such situations is on the social planners and the initiatives of government and professional agencies. To say that lives are barren and sterile is to say that these lives are oriented to that which is barren and sterile. If we are to be active agents in the world, to make history rather than be passive observers of events, then we must choose the themes of our story. Those themes will in turn give coherence to our lives and significantly shape our view of reality. Action depends on the vision of the world we would create, vision depends on character, and character is the shape of the dramatic patterns and themes of our story. In the individual these patterns and themes make character. In society as a whole they make culture. When the patterns of our culture, the objects of our attention are professional methodologies, engineered technologies, large-scale industrial production, and the acquisition of its output, then to take our attention elsewhere is a task of the first magnitude, requiring an inner transformation. Wendell Berry offers a beautiful description of a transformed focus of attention.

People are joined to the land by work. Land, work, people and community are all comprehended in the idea of culture. These connections cannot be understood or described by information— so many resources to be transformed by so many workers into so many products for so many consumers—because they are not quantitative. We can understand them only after we acknowledge that they should be harmonious—that a culture must be either shapely and saving or shapeless and destructive. To presume to describe land, work, people and community in information, by quantities, seems invariably to throw them into competition with one another.[15]

The reader should not misunderstand the thrust of this discussion. In the effort to create and sustain a harmonious family we have many times made extensive use of the best professional help available. Nothing is being said about placing reason on the shelf or discarding knowledge. Nor should one translate "harmonious" in this instance to mean "placid and tranquil." The issue is a commitment to a new focus of enduring, caring, loving attention upon delicate interdependencies; to learning how to feel in one's bones when relationships are right and when they are going wrong. The knowledge of those helping professionals, whether they be therapists, clergy, counselors, or teachers, is simply an abstraction, until it becomes particular in the harmonies of our lives. Such commitment will require the discipline to focus attention on the intricate notes and chords of family life. There is no other path to literacy in the harmonies of a good family.

A system is by nature interdependent. When any one link goes bad it all starts to go bad. By tending to those links, as a good farmer tends to the fields, through a disciplined attention characterized by qualities like steadfastness, hope, and love, one learns the harmonies of the essential relationships. Technology can, for a time, substitute for those harmonies, but only for a time. When it fails, as it must, we are left illiterate, unable to know what is good and right and proper. What is it that makes good people—good families? And what makes good families—good communities? And what makes good communities—good people? The way to know what that means is to tend those relationships, to make them the object of our attention, the themes of our story.

4. The Small Community and the Mediating System

Author Willie Morris wrote an article recently entitled "Now That I Am Fifty." He recounts what was important to him in earlier years and then speaks of what is important now. "As I age, it is not the grandiose equations that abide, but family, friendship, community. It is important for me to feel at one with a beloved place, its cadences and continuities."[1]

No one lives in American society today in total self-sufficiency—absolutely no one. From the time we come into the world from the wombs of our mothers until death and the burial of our remains, we live in relation to and are dependent on other people. While some may attempt isolation and total self-sufficiency for a period of their lives, it is never achieved fully.

We are not only dependent upon family and those immediately around us. The family, neighborhood, region, nation, and the world are different, if only ever so slightly, because each of us is here. You are one more mouth to feed, body to clothe, and life to take care of. You are also one more actor arranging and rearranging the physical and social environment of the world.

We all suffer or benefit from the wheat harvest in the Great Plains, the water shortage in the Southwest, the decision by Congress and the president to build MX missiles, the famine in Africa, the apartheid system in South Africa, the technological advances of the Japanese, the new awakening of China, and terrorist activity in Lebanon. Every person born, every shot fired, every breakthrough in science, every child kidnapped affects every other life directly, indirectly, or in terms of what might have been.

The major issues of humankind seem to be the big ones— regional, national, or world issues. They are the ones reported by the large radio and TV networks and the metropolitan and regional newspapers—war, terrorism, assassinations, hunger, tax reform, the plight of small farmers, revolutions, political alliances, changing systems of health care, abortion, and inflation. Each of us is affected by and cares about all of these. Closer to home, the local news media talk about crime, illegal drugs, crop failures, bank failures, a new convention center, transportation systems, and prison overcrowding. These issues also limit or provide opportunities for each of us.

While some of us prefer not to think about our personal investment and involvement in these and hundreds of similar concerns, most of us know when we consider the implications that we participate in the consequences. And most of us care. Would that we were able to reach out and touch, to respond with healing and help, or participate in providing solutions or encouragement.

Few of these issues lend themselves to easy involvement by us average folk—laypeople who have not been certified as experts in these fields. Even if we do persevere and work our way into involvement with an issue, we question the worth of it all. The issues are so complex, and so political, and so *big*.

These are not the only issues. Closer to home and in our personal lives there are so many more. From our individual perspectives there are the real dilemmas of everyday living—protecting our property, getting street lights replaced and garbage collected, getting a job, getting along with the boss, passing an examination, coping with divorce, responding to the illness or death of a friend, or getting out of debt. These are the challenges Joan faced in taking responsibility for the elderly living in a retirement home, or Fran in her concern about her value in the community, intimate relationship with God, others, and her grandchildren, and tracing socks and pencils.

Answers to the questions of daily life are not always easy to find either. Some of these issues may respond to a disciplined effort. Others, however, seem as far out of reach as tax reform and world peace. Even when we want to respond, individual effort may not be enough, and how to involve oneself with others is not readily apparent.

In short, we do not live in the world alone. Our individual lives are intertwined with those of others. Both meeting the challenges of everyday life and pursuing the quest for self-fulfillment are accomplished as we join in productive and meaning-filled relationships with fellow travelers—those who share our dilemmas and our mission for a better life and a better world.

Philip Slater says,

Urban and suburban Americans do not live in communities, they live in networks. A network is an address book—a list of people who may have little in common besides oneself. Each network has only one reference point that defines it. No two people have the same precise network. This means that everyone controls her own social milieu, and if she likes can subsist entirely on interpersonal candy bars. The persons in her network do not know each other, so she is never forced to integrate the disparate sides of herself but can compartmentalize them in disconnected relationships.[2]

It is our belief that the first task in the quest for human wholeness and good societies is people finding the appropriate others for the journey. While each of us have family and friends, they may not be the ones, or the only ones, who share concern for the issues, the vision, or the context to form the alliances that will render our skills and efforts productive. But it is clear that more than disjointed networks are needed. The neighborhood or small community where one lives is the primary setting for achieving wholeness, and our neighbors are our best potential allies in the task of moral development, of dealing effectively with community, national, and world issues, and building good societies. The neighborhood, its people, and its institutions—families, schools, churches, businesses, political organizations—can be the mediating system between individual efforts and a better world.

MEDIATING SYSTEM

Viewing the bewildering array of issues and processes that surround us and shape us, we begin to see that we live in two complementary and interdependent worlds—our private world and the public world. Private and public refer to domains of life and activity. In our private domains we own and control property for our own benefit and may exclude others at will. In the public sphere property is owned in common and maintained for the common good; no one may be excluded due to personal characteristics such as race, class, creed, or color. In our private lives we decide and act at will. In public our individual decisions are limited, and we are obliged to act according to rules. Private matters are of an intimate or confidential nature, while public matters are open and deal with civic interests.

The ironic dilemma of society in the modern world is that the private and public domains have come to limit each other rather than nurture and sustain each other. These two spheres have become divorced in a way that negates symbiotic support. The individual in his or her private world has lost the power to know and act responsibly in the public world. Conversely, the public domain so controls the structures and processes of our private lives that individuals believe themselves to be powerless to act even in matters of a private nature. We feel that our personal lives have been invaded by big bureaucracies, and we feel helpless as private citizens to influence their direction and control.

Since we cannot live as private people alone in the world,

and since on the other hand we value the freedom to control our own destinies, it is imperative that we discover the bridge between our private and public worlds that will enable us to live effectively in both domains, realizing that they truly are interdependent. If wholeness is what we seek, we have no other choice.

The concept of a mediating system between our private and public worlds is, we believe, the only answer. This mediating system is made up of structures and institutions that have served us in the past and continue in place but no longer function in a mediating and conciliating role.

Peter Berger provides the basic definition of the mediating system when he speaks of those structures "that stand between the individual in his private sphere and the large institutions of a modern society. In this location, mediating structures are, as it were, Janus-faced: on the one hand, they provide meaning and identity to personal life; on the other hand, they insure that the large institutions, notably the state, do not lose their connection with *personal meanings*."[3]

Figure 5 shows the role and relationships of such a system. The individual in her or his private world is depicted on the left. The public sphere with its large-scale institutions of government, communications, economics, and education is shown at right. The lines between the two worlds represent the attempts by both sectors to reach, influence, and support each other. As the diagram shows, however, this is not happening in our society today. Somewhere in between is the "right level" of structures and institutions that can be developed to function in a mediating role. This system of structures needs to be near enough to give the individual some sense of belonging and some possibility of influence and control. Yet it must also have sufficient proximity to the institutions of power in the public sphere to influence them and make a difference. As indicated in the figure, a functioning mediating system will consist of a

Figure 5. The Individual's Relationship to the Institutions of Modern Society

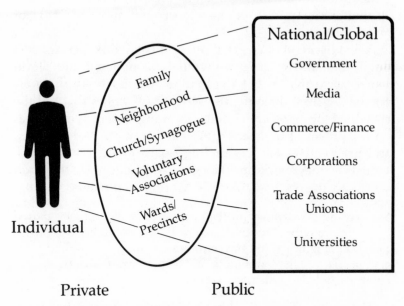

small community or neighborhood in which people live and the primary social institutions within those communities that bring people together in mutually beneficial and productive ways—family, church, local political institutions such as wards and precincts, and other voluntary associations such as clubs and self-help groups. No one or two of these mediating structures can accomplish the task alone. The neighborhood, together with its institutions, is the primary unit of mediating power. If this neighborhood system itself cannot move toward wholeness, it cannot accomplish wholeness for individuals and the larger society. On the other hand, whole integrated neighborhoods with families, churches, and political and social organizations moving together toward a citizen-initiated-and-owned vision of the good life are the building blocks for good societies and a good world. They are also the contexts in which individuals may work out life patterns that are satisfying, integrated, and capable of continuous renewal of good societies.

A mediating system that functions to link private and public domains relating individuals to national and world issues performs several roles. It establishes through interpersonal citizen dialogue the virtues and values that will be cherished by people. It offers meaning-based perspectives on life processes and activities. The common goals, values, and perspectives are a sounding board or mirror for individuals as they work out the goals and values that they will set for their own lives. Arthur Morgan comments:

> Society and government in their larger units will not be moved by any more refined motives, and will have no higher objectives, than do the families and the communities from which their leadership arises. The community is the mother of society. As the community is, so will society be.[4]

The vision of one neighborhood interacts with the vision of all other neighborhoods to build a society from the bottom up. As individuals and small communities participate in setting the standards for the state and the world, they become invested in the quality of life for all who dwell on the earth. Their investment is in goals that they have helped to shape; and through their own neighborhood's participation with other neighborhoods they have, and feel that they have, direct involvement in the achievement of those goals.

An efficient mediating system then facilitates both the shaping of vision and the empowerment to act. There is more. A mediating system provides skill training in manageable units for individuals and groups who want to participate in building or rebuilding a good society, but who need a place to begin and knowledge to act productively. A mediating system also provides network supports for citizens so that they have adequate information, access, and emotional support in this work.

Mass institutions cannot offer these simple but necessary tools for such movement to begin or continue. Neither are they readily accessible to individuals who alone may lack experience, encouragement, or craftiness (political savvy).

A mediating system operates both ways. It directs its benefits to the individual and to the mass structures of society. It has the opportunity to offer the strengths and achievements of one to the weaknesses and failures of the other. It can be the catalyst for enabling good people at every level of political organization, but the key level is the small community.

THE SMALL COMMUNITY

We have seen in the preceding chapter that the primary agent for establishing and reinforcing the resources and values for good people is the family. We have seen also that the family is the institution that is most likely to lead the way in reestablishing an operational good-people system. But families, like individuals, do not exist in isolation from the social setting in which family members participate individually and together with other people to pursue and achieve common objectives—learning, earning a living, maintaining safety, and finding meaning. This common social setting for the family is a neighborhood or small community, terms used here interchangeably.

In a rural area, a neighborhood or small community may cover several square miles but encompass only a few families and a store, church, or school. In the city, a neighborhood is the smallest operating unit above family or block club.

It is the arena where a variety of human relationships develop from people living close together. As Lewis Mumford has written, "Neighbors are people united primarily not by common origins or common purposes but by the proximity of their dwellings in space. . . . There is nothing forced in this relationship and to be real it need not be deep: a nod, a friendly word, a recognized face, an uttered name—this is all that is needed to establish and preserve in some fashion the sense of belonging together."[5]

A neighborhood is more than a network of friends or acquaintances—it is a place—a place from which family members may go out and to which they can return. During their adult years, some people may live in the neighborhood but not work or seek their recreation there. Even so the neighborhood is a familiar place that one knows and understands. For most it is home—almost as much as the family house is home. A personal reminiscence captures the flavor of how this is so.

I recently returned to the neighborhood where I grew up and lived until graduation from college. My mother still lives in that neighborhood in the same house. I had been back many times during the twenty-five years since leaving to live in other places—other neighborhoods. I had gone back to visit the family. On those visits, through letters and in telephone conversations with the family, I had kept up with many changes in the neighborhood—who had married, had children, died, or moved away. I had heard the stories of those who made good and those who had not—also the stories of who had been good and who had not. And of course I had seen for myself some of the physical changes in the community as I had driven in and out.

On my recent visit, however, I saw the old neighborhood again with time for reflection as I went for a long walk. I remembered how much a part of me this neighborhood really was and is even today.

None of the "original" families on our block were still there—that is, "original" from my perspective—those who lived there when I arrived on the scene and remembered as a child. Most had died. It had been a well-kept, lower-middle-class community except for one house up on the corner. The continuing parade of families who lived in that house all seemed to be different than the rest of us—trashy, lazy, lower morals—or so we thought. That house was in better repair than I had ever seen it, but nobody lived there just now.

Mrs. Allen, our next-door neighbor, outlived most of her family, but she died several years ago. Her daughter now lives in her big house alone. Mrs. Allen was one of the nicest people in the area—saintly, caring—a good person.

On up the street was the Davis house. Johnny and I often played together and Mrs. Davis would cut my hair in her kitchen for only 50 cents when it cost a dollar at the barber shop. Across from them was the Land house. They were the last people to have chickens in their backyard. I would go each week to their house to buy eggs. Mrs. Land and another neighbor Mrs. Hall were the ones I could most count on to buy figs from me when money was short in the summertime.

I walked on up and down the streets remembering. The neighborhood school was only a block from my home. The building looks the same. Only one of the teachers lived in the neighborhood, but she came after I was past the grade she taught. Looking back, I think most of the teachers at this school were good people. They surely did have a lot of patience with me and "my crowd." I guess they understood children and realized that we would probably amount to something someday if people like themselves did not give up on us. I feel bad about the way I treated them sometimes. I really wish it were possible to tell them that and thank them.

The little white store across from the school has been torn down. Mr. Sparks, the owner, sold every kind of candy and gum one can imagine. He made a comfortable living until he died of a heart attack. I worked for him part time. I was there when the news came that he would not be back. I have always wished I could ask his forgiveness for the ice cream sandwich I ate but did not pay for. No one else was ever able to make a go of that little store.

The church was three blocks away. It became the center of my life, although there were long stretches as a teenager when I did not attend regularly. Our Boy Scout troop met there too. As I walked through the neighborhood I was particularly struck by the fond memories of Sunday school class socials and the teachers who were always there and always had trouble keeping order so that they could teach us something. I am sure each one was glad when my class moved on, but they sure acted as though they would miss us.

Many other community landmarks were still there—Little Park where we played baseball, Hollow Park where we had a wading pool, Fair Park where there were rides and an amusement center, two other churches, and the multi-neighborhood shopping center at the edge of the community. Gone were the fire station, two drugstores, another small grocery store, and the marble works where they made tombstones. Changed was the racial makeup and social status of the community and the condition of houses and yards. New was the post office, swimming pool in Hollow Park, another Baptist church, neighborhood self-help organizations, and many, many apartment buildings.

As I walked the streets of the old neighborhood, I had the feeling that I was home. All of it was home. As a youngster this was all my turf, and I belonged to a lot of people who lived there. What I mean is there were many people in that community who knew me and seemed to care that I behaved and that I would "do something" with my life—be somebody.

Individuals and families do not live in isolation; that is, unless they choose to, and even then they really do not. There are few people in our society who do not have a home base of some sort somewhere as the primary place of living—a house, an apartment, condominium, tent, or room. Most such places are in a small community of some type. Our interest here is the nature of that community, the quality of life there, how people relate to it and to one another, and whether the basic needs of families and individuals find fulfillment there.

The experience of growing up in a neighborhood like the one described is not really typical. There are no typical or textbook communities. At the same time some communities today have many of the same characteristics as that one.

It is obvious, however, that the nature of American life, including community life, has changed.

In many neighborhoods the dynamics of community life—the fabric that holds us together—have been broken. Some time ago a small community inherited a five-acre parcel of land. A debate immediately ensued between the political leaders and local residents about how the property would be used. The mayor and city commissioners suggested selling the land for private housing. The local residents asked that the land be reserved for a park. The mayor responded that a park would be costly to establish and maintain and that money was not budgeted for that purpose. There was also a fear that a park might be used for drug dealing. After much discussion, an unofficial public referendum was called. The town newsletter carried a ballot and the following news item:

Real estate authorities believe that a city park has a direct downward effect, in adjacent areas, on residential values. The City of _____ has made every effort to protect and assure property values through careful zoning and regulatory ordinances. For many years, _____ has been a stable residential community, thereby protecting property values. The Commissioners feel that it is their responsibility to keep the present stability, thereby continuing to protect the value of residential property.

The park lost 513 to 111.

Wholesome and productive community life requires public places where people can meet and relate. In this and many neighborhoods few such places remain. We force people into their homes through lack of public arenas for interchange with little awareness that we have cut off the possibility for neighborly interaction.

For the last quarter-century, neighborhoods have been fluid, with upwardly mobile pople moving out, leaving behind those who are, for one reason or another, less able to care for themselves. In response to this, government and private responsibility has been motivated to provide services—health clinics, community recreation centers, day-care centers for the very young and the very old. There are also many examples of community advocacy groups that seek to influence government policy. Except in affluent areas, from which private schools draw their students, children usually attend neighborhood schools until they are twelve or thirteen; then they begin to journey out of the immediate area for schooling. Even where churches are true neighborhood institutions their efforts are concentrated on their members rather than on the community as a whole, except perhaps in occasional outreach programs. In none of this effort has there been any sustained effort to use the greatest resource any neighborhood has to improve the quality of life—namely, the people themselves. Instead of being regarded as the source of service to each other they are more often regarded as recipients of service provided by either volunteers or government or some corporation.

There may at last be in our day forces beginning to work at changing the situation. A tightened economy has discouraged home buying, causing people to remain in the same dwellings; high energy and automobile costs have made traveling long distances to work unattractive for many; disintegrating public transit systems in our cities have reduced mobility, particularly in working-class communities. This means that upwardly mobile people are beginning to remain in their neighborhoods. Where this is not already happening it should be encouraged, for if people remain in their neighborhoods as change takes place, the leadership will not be drained off to other communities. In such cases, the change is often not as radical, and there is no long wait for new leaders to emerge.

Communities do not lack people of goodwill; often, however, these people lack the skills, information, and leadership to undertake intentional service to others. Little in our general education gives us the basic skills and knowledge needed for Christian citizenship in society today. But within a given neighborhood there are resources to improve the quality of life that go unused for lack of coordination, networking, and adequate direction. Where resources and services are lacking, they can be taught or acquired.

If it is an underprivileged neighborhood, we have the word of Harry Spence, court-appointed receiver of the bankrupt Boston Housing Authority, that "the issue is not poverty. The real issue is social membership. People can live poor if they have some sense of participation in the larger community."[6] At the other end of the scale, in affluent neighborhoods, people often live in loneliness, isolation, fear, and separation. They too can do something about it.

Neighborhoods are properly informal structures that should serve a mediating role between the private spheres of life and the domain of the large institutional, bureaucratic, governmental, and corporate enterprises that hold sway over so much of modern life. It is through these mediating structures that individuals are helped or not helped in negotiating the transitions between life as the private individual and public life as a productive member of society.

Many in our day have succumbed to the temptation to withdraw from community life and adopt a private outlook on the world. They have attempted to care for their personal needs with only the help of scattered friends. They have assumed that community beyond the family is no longer possible. The inability to find ways to participate in public affairs has led to the conclusion that there is not a legitimate and necessary role there for average citizens.

It is obvious that the mediating power and importance of the neighborhood varies across the ages and stages of the lifespan. Children and the elderly tend to have greater needs for the mediation of neighborhood structures, but all people in our society need the opportunity to be attached in loving and helping ways with other people who share, if nothing else, a common place. We believe that a focus on intentional service by people at the neighborhood level can bring about the grass roots development of social systems, which will lead to greater effective cooperation among the mediating structures and hence a higher quality of life for those involved. "It is only in a society in which most individuals take responsibility for their quality of life, rather than passively receive it, that continuous improvement of it can be realized."[7]

In a given locale the quality of life depends on the cooperative interrelationships among the neighborhood and upon the varieties and types of mediating structures within the neighborhood. Unfortunately, families, churches, and voluntary associations tend to operate autonomously and privately, as if they are closed systems operating apart from the neighborhood.

Along with families, the primary mediating structures, including the church and voluntary self-help groups, seem to have the most power to initiate cooperation and to involve the people of a neighborhood in functionally useful endeavors to raise the quality of life.

COMMUNITY INSTITUTIONS

As we have seen, neighborhoods or small communities are formed as individuals and families locate in the same geographical area. Coming together in a neighborhood is rarely intentional; that is, people seldom determine in advance that they will inhabit the same area and live in relationship as families. Notable exceptions are national, ethnic, or racial groups who are settling outside their native country. Each wave of immigrants to the United States tended to settle in close proximity to one another at first—at least until they could overcome language and other cultural barriers. Some groups, such as the Amish, have continued in intentional, close-knit, exclusive communities for generations. Most, however, begin to disperse throughout other communities by the second generation.

But most neighborhoods today are formed by people

who do not have previous ties and who have chosen the area for other reasons. As they come together in neighborhoods, families do have something in common—the necessity of learning to live in relationship. In addition to personal and family needs for which they may agree to seek fulfillment together, sharing babysitting or lawn tools, a whole new range of needs and possibilities for cooperation is presented. A new setting is created by the coming together of two or more people in close proximity, and the new setting, the neighborhood in this case, takes on a life of its own. Cooperation remains optional in some regards—creation of parks and libraries, street lighting, and garbage disposal—with neighbors deciding to act in concert or leaving each family free to meet the need in its own way. In other areas, concerted cooperative action is mandatory. Protection against pestilence and common enemies and maintenance of safety and stability for each individual demand some degree of cooperation, at least at times, if the community is to endure.

In between the purely optional and the mandatory areas of community responsibility are dozens of possibilities for neighborhood citizens to act together for the common good. They may covenant and act together in two-family units, block groups, associations of interested individuals, task forces, or all together to establish schools, churches, civic clubs, recreational organizations, safety patrols, self-help groups, hospitals, single-purpose public authorities, and similar institutions. It is conceivable that a given community could exist without any of these structures. In this case socialization into community life, the practice of religion, entertainment, health services, and the like remain the responsibility of each family unit.

The fact is that few communities in American life since our nation's founding have opted to leave such important functions totally to the care of individual households. Because these aspects of our lives are by their very nature relational, families have chosen to establish associational or institutional structures to supplement familial efforts. Two points here are especially important.

First, responsibility for safety, education, religion, health, value formation, and other quality-of-life factors are and always will be the primary responsibility of the family. Community efforts can only supplement, reinforce, and extend the care offered within the primary social unit of the home. This fact does not lessen the importance of community activity. Rather it reinforces the significance of uniting the building blocks to form a larger entity. It is the same principle as strong neighborhoods creating healthy societies. Neighborhoods, as the chief mediating structures between private individuals and the public institutions, can function effectively only so long as the quality of family life is maintained.

Second, this analysis of neighborhoods reminds us that schools, churches, hospitals, and civic associations are not self-generating. They are given life and sustained by the corporate will of a community. They cannot exist apart from the community. If the community brought these institutions into existence they must render a service for the common good. If they serve well, their offerings directly or indirectly benefit the entire neighborhood. If they fail in their task, the whole neighborhood suffers and the quality of life for all is diminished.

Institutions, associations, and processes given birth by and sustained for the benefit of a neighborhood or small community are by definition public entities. While they may respond to such deeply personal needs as expansion of the mind in education, faith development in religion, or the functioning of one's body in health, the public nature of the structure offering the service must be understood and maintained. As we have said before, public means open to all, for the common good, community ownership.

It is, of course, possible that one or more individuals within a community may create a private structure to serve some or all of the people in a neighborhood. Most businesses are private entities, for example. The services they render or products they sell may be very important, even necessary to the health and functioning of the community. The business may respond to needs for food, transportation, communication, clothing, or shelter—all important to the quality of life in the neighborhood. Some may even create private schools or private clubs and restrict the people who are allowed to participate. Increasingly, the long-time public province of health care, including hospitals, has been entered by the private sector. The same is true in the area of telephone service, garbage collection, and recreation.

The replacement of traditional public services and institutions by private ones has even pervaded organized, community-generated religious institutions. Certain sects and religious groups have long functioned as private movements, excluding all but those who have been initiated, accept right doctrine, pay the required fee, or act in a specified way. Such groups generally are organized apart from the neighborhood and function to draw from it rather than give to it.

Over the years, various ordinances or ceremonies of the church have been privatized—baptisms, weddings, funerals, naming ceremonies, and the like. In some cases, private chapels have been built for these traditional congregational functions. A more serious trend in religion, however, is the tendency of churches to forget their community origins, to disregard community responsibilities and seek adherents and participants on the basis of specialized programming—many times seeking members who look, think, and act alike and hence will enjoy being together in church. In this case, the church becomes a private institution, and the character of the neighborhood population is ignored. Also ignored is the responsibility of the church toward the religious and moral life of the community. Peter L. Berger and Richard John Neuhaus point out that

although specifically religious activities have been largely privatized, the first part of the proposition overlooks the complex ways
in which essentially religious values infiltrate and influence our
public thought. But even to the extent that the first part of the
proposition is true, it does not follow that religion is therefore
irrelevant to public policy. The family, for example, is intimately
involved in the institution of religion, and since the family is one
of the prime mediating structures (perhaps the prime one), this
makes the church urgently relevant to public policy. Without
falling into the trap of politicizing all of life, our point is that
structures such as family, church, and neighborhood are all public
institutions in the sense that they must be taken seriously in the
ordering of the policy.[8]

We do not object to private enterprise in business or in
social services—even those that have historically grown out
of the life of a small community and served the common
good of the community. Some services may well be lodged
in either private or public sectors while some are best lodged
in the private domain. We would argue, however, that the
neighborhood is the appropriate level in our society to
mediate the gap that has developed between individuals and
families, on the one hand, and large institutions and global
human issues, on the other. We believe that neighborhoods
together with families as anchors for mediating systems
composed of schools, churches, and other primary social
institutions initiated by community action are essential to
the reform and maintenance of the good-people system in
our society. In this sense the mediating system and all its
derivative components must be self-consciously public—for
both the individual and common good.

THE CHURCH

Churches, synagogues, and other religious institutions
(referred to collectively here as "churches") make up the
largest group of voluntary associations in American society.

"It is perhaps relevant to understanding American society to note that on any given Sunday there are probably more people in churches than the total number of people who attend professional sports events in a whole year—or to note that there are close to 500,000 local churches and synagogues voluntarily supported by the American people."[9] No other institution in the nation has been treated with the high degree of respect and privilege they have been afforded both legally and consensually. Churches have been given the role of helping individuals confront the issues of meaning and purpose, of undergirding family life, of positing hope in times of crisis, of shaping individual and relational values, of leading moral crusades, and of providing a base of integrity in political and social relationships.

Within the family, and between the family and the larger society, the church is a primary agent for bearing and transmitting the operative values of our society. This is true not only in the sense that most Americans identify their most important values as being religious in character, but also in the sense that the values that inform our public discourse are inseparably related to specific religious traditions. In the absence of the church and other mediating structures that articulate these values, the result is not that the society is left without operative values; the result is that the state has an unchallenged monopoly on the generation and maintenance of values.[10]

The time-honored separation of religious and political structures has been carefully preserved as the foundation of freedom and decency in public life. This does not mean that one sphere is private and the other public. Rather it is because both church and state have been able to operate independently and complementarily within the public realm that the desired results have been achieved. "Institutions of religion should be unfettered to make their maximum contribution to the public interest. In some areas of social service and education, this means these institutions should be free [and encouraged] to continue doing what they have historically done."[11]

The church has also served communities traditionally as the foremost initiator of other voluntary organizations to care for community needs. "In the public policy areas . . . health, social welfare, education, and so on—the historical development of programs, ideas, and institutions is inseparable from the church."[12] Most if not all voluntary associations on the public scene today, and many private ones, can trace their origins to the church. The church in its responsibility for integrating all of life in frameworks of meaning has consistently monitored the community for new needs and new opportunities to bring about a better life for the citizenry.

It is in these two roles of moral conscience and creator of new possibilities that the church has made and continues to make community life better. And it is in these roles that the church participates together with family and neighborhood as a significant component of the mediating system.

If the church is to make its best contribution in this regard, it will reinvest itself in the neighborhood that spawned it and turn its attention "to the way people order their lives and values at the most local and concrete levels of their existence."[13] It will establish as its primary referent the common good of the community in which it is located rather than the strength of its own life or its standing in the denomination. Rather than viewing its neighborhood and other neighborhoods as reservoirs from which to draw members and resources to serve the congregation's ends, it will prepare itself to give its best gifts to all the people (members and nonmembers) who inhabit its geographical area. Competition with other neighborhood congregations and community institutions will yield to forceful and intentional cooperation toward the common end of a more loving and just community. It may even be helpful for some churches to stop keeping membership rolls so that they are not tempted to divide the neighborhood population into "us" and "them." And the churches will encourage member participation in community life through nonaffiliated associations, recognizing and rewarding people for community activity as well as church activity.

Regrettably, these actions will require changes in the modus operandi of most religious institutions today. With few exceptions churches have turned their focus inward and are assuming falsely that building strong churches will in some undetermined way produce good communities. We believe the opposite is true. To identify ends that are proximate rather than final is to guarantee that the institution will not go beyond its identified goals. If churches are to contribute to their communities as important partners in mediating systems, they must share the whole vision with the other components of the system.

In a recent article, noted church-planning specialist Lyle Schaller has argued that the lack of identification by churches with their communities and hence with their origins and nature as public institutions is a result of the cultural shift in America from an agricultural society to an urban one— a movement that has brought even small towns and sparsely populated rural areas into the urban domain.

In the early years of this century, much of the continuity in the typical Protestant church in agricultural America was in the kinship ties that bound members together and the fact that many members saw one another several times during the course of the typical week. This continuity also was reinforced by the attachment to place, loyalty to that denominational family, the cemetery located next to the meeting house and the interdependence of neighbors.

The urbanization of the American population has eroded those strands. When today's congregation is examined as a social institution, a much larger share of the continuity is in the pastor, the program, the building and, perhaps, the group life of that church.

In other words, the church has turned inward and as a

private organization focuses on its own life. Schaller goes on:

A second change has been the shift from a geographical or nationality defined role of the parish to an identity reflected in the distinctive characteristics of the ministry and program, personality of the pastor, building, or common characteristics of the members.

In urban America outsiders may identify a congregation as "the new Korean congregation that was organized a couple of years ago" or "a blue-collar parish" or "Dr. Harrison's church" or "the church with the great choir." Far less common are references based upon the place of residence or denominational affiliation.

In agricultural America the place of work, residence, schooling, worship and the place to meet and make friends usually was the same community. It could be defined geographically, often by school district boundaries. . . .

Within that social context it was easy and effective to use a geographical definition of the parish boundaries. . . . Today, about the only urban congregations that can use a geographical definition of their parish boundaries are the new congregations ministering to first owners of single family residences.[14]

This is an accurate analysis of what has occurred in the American church scene, and Schaller has identified a major cause, or at least a major coincidental trend, that has reinforced the failure of churches to identify with their geographical communities.

We take issue with Schaller, however, regarding what should be done. He seems to suggest as a solution that the church accommodate itself to the changes that have occurred. He says: "The most obvious is the need for longer pastorates. . . . More significant is the shift from the neighborhood to the work place as the primary point of socialization. This requires a new conceptual model for describing the central characteristics of a congregation."[15]

A far better solution would be the re-creation of neighborhoods and the reconnection of people with the institutions that give order to their lives. The loss of community orientation by the church is symptomatic of what has occurred within most public institutions. The result has been the loss of supportive community for many people—particularly the very young, the disadvantaged, and the elderly—for families, and for all of us. Rather than accept the trend and accommodate themselves to community fragmentation and citizen alienation, churches should help neighborhoods rediscover their place in American society.

The church may again be the best institution in the mediating system, and in society as a whole, to initiate and guide the process of community reformulation. It may be the only one. Local governments do not know there is a problem; state and national governments are too far removed. Schools have already been removed from many small communities. Chambers of commerce are too specialized. Families are struggling for their own survival, and self-help groups tend to be focused on single issues.

Indeed the church may be the catalyst. The parish church or synagogue is still in many places a neighbor-centered institution. It may become one in many more. There is a congregation in almost every community, and studies show they are usually respected and admired. Each congregation can offer the gift of its laity to this task. No other institution is so well situated to play such a key role in the mediating system. The question is whether the churches can reorient their own lives—take their eyes off themselves and look around them.

5. Repair and Transformation

How can we care for our world, ourselves, and our neighbors so that the results are good and so that good can in turn compound the good for all? That is the question. If current vision of the answer is blurred and confused, it is in part because our attention has been misdirected, diverted onto false paths until the ordinary citizen is left muddled and passive in the face of problems that seem unreachable and intractable.

To get a manageable handle on this question seems all but impossible amidst all the messages of the TV, newspapers, magazines, and other stimuli. Try for a moment to bring the problem down to a scale and context we all can understand and appreciate.

A MOUNTAIN HOME METAPHOR

Imagine that you have retired and you have taken savings and purchased a small, rundown cabin in the mountains. Your new home is on a small pond fed by a brook rising from a spring located on the edge of your property. You could afford to buy the property because previous owners had so mistreated the land that no one wanted it. The road leading to your place was bulldozed, and rain and erosion left the road impassable and the brook choked with silt. The property once contained a grove of large, beautiful redwood trees. These were cut down and sold by the previous owner. The destruction of the grove increased erosion, caused the silting of the pond, and left a small meadow in ruts and gouges from the traffic of a four-wheel truck used to haul out the logs. A defective septic tank, the silt, the choked brook have combined to ruin the water in the small lake. You have been told by the one neighbor on the lake who will deign to talk with you that relationships with the previous owner became so bad that his truck was burned in a mysterious midnight fire. This rusted hulk still sits in a corner of the furrowed meadow. The issue is how to care for this property, for yourself and family, and for your neighbors in such a way as to give good results, to the end that the good can compound and provide good for all.

Let your imagination work on this example and let it inform the way you focus your attention and vision.

Perhaps the first thing to notice is that, even if one had the resources, there is no way to fix everything at one time. Hope rests in the direction of patient repair by small increments. And yet each small repair, if it is to be good, cannot be regarded as a solitary act. It must be a part of a process in harmony with the patterns that in concert create a good environment. A repair on a rut in the road must take into account the natural drainage of the land, the runoff into the brook, the need to restore water quality, ease of access to neighbors, and so on. What you do will not be good if it resolves one problem at the expense of another. But if the action you take is correct it will not only help to repair the road, it will act inevitably to help correct the larger whole— waterflow through the brook, water quality in the lake, relationships with the neighbors, the regeneration of the acquatic life, which in turn will help to raise the water quality, which then increases the goodwill of the neighbors. If you were to rely on experts you would need, just to begin, a botanist, a marine biologist, a road construction engineer, a social psychologist, a naturalist, and a waste-water treatment specialist. Moreover the whole situation has a historical element. There is a past story to be dealt with, neighbors moving on, the flux of natural forces and new events, all to be comprehended in the whole.

The pattern of the whole system is unbelievably complex and interdependent. You must act; and yet to act unwisely will make what is already bad worse. Where will the wisdom come from? From a reasoned, intuitive vision of the whole, which is fashioned in a thousand small acts of devoted repair, each taken with patience and a disciplined attention to the harmonies and patterns of land, water, and people. In this situation, you and the land and the water and your neighbors will all be transformed. Your repair of past misdeeds doesn't just restore things, it leads to a good system, new and different, of land and people. The responsibility in this situation is yours and yours alone. Knowing what to do requires learning all that you can, delving fully into the pain of the past, letting your imagination form a vision of the future, and then acting on that vision in countless small acts of repair, each of which serves to overcome the competing, fragmenting, nonharmonious forces at work.[1]

Through this story there are many elements of the situation in which we all live. As a good neighbor parable, the story expresses the fact that we must and can act to be good neighbors in the creation of a good society. As a metaphor, the story organizes and demonstrates the overall pattern of transformative repair possible for each of us in our own diverse environments. One of the reasons for choosing this story as a metaphor for individual action and responsibility is that its scale and perspective are right. When one reads of massive social problems such as the breakdown of the family, the rise in crime, or the prevalence of child abuse, one is overwhelmed by the magnitude and unreachable nature of such issues. We have been conditioned to the role of passive observers, as if living in society were like taking a cruise on a great ocean liner whose rusting hull, inept crew, failing engines, and faulty navigation are utterly beyond our control or comprehension.

It is more appropriate to focus on the multitude of individual stitches woven into the fabric of society, to look at the threads of social and physical relationships spun into the intricate web of our culture. Each of us can and must contribute to the making of the web, making it more resilient and beautiful. The slender threads of our lives can repair places where the web has been torn or where gaps exist. Whether we live on a rural farm or in an urban highrise, our attention should be upon the remarkable tapestry of the fabric of the world about us. As in the metaphor of the mountain home, no one will be able to tend the situation for us, no one else can contribute what you have to give. One's vision of the whole, a physical presence, the knowledge that comes only from having lived in and cared for such a situation, and the sustained continuity of our personal actions are gifts that uniquely belong to each of us. No one else can contribute these gifts for us, and yet no other gifts are more important for the transformative repair of the good-people system.

With the mountain home example to guide us, we will look more closely at some of the important gaps in our society where the need and the possibility for transformative repair are possible. We want to look at some of the specific gaps in the good-people system and at some of the possibilities for their repair.

THE GAP BETWEEN SOCIAL ILLS AND SOCIAL SERVICE PROVIDERS

Suppose that you are elderly, living by yourself, having to watch every penny, but you are rather fiercely independent. You've been ill, and now you find yourself skimping on food. Money is scarce, transportation is difficult, the larder is not always full, so it's easier to heat a can of soup or skip a meal than to go through all the steps necessary to shop for and cook a full dinner. You are aware that the county office on aging runs some form of nutrition or supplemental feeding program. How likely is it that you would turn to it for assistance?

The answer for many people depends on the degree to which they are a part of a network of natural helpers. By natural helpers we mean friends, family, neighbors:

- who are available, who reside close at hand
- who have some experiential knowledge of the relevant problem you are facing
- who are trusted because they listen, care, and know their limits

In addition, natural helping networks will often draw in intermediate helpers such as the neighborhood pharmacist, the mail carrier, the clergy, local shopkeepers; persons whose work and activity keep them close at hand and whose way of relating includes natural friendship. Natural helping networks depend on availability, empathy, trust, experiential knowledge, and on relationships between peers. The experience of longstanding mutual help organizations like Alcoholics Anonymous suggests that among natural helpers a shared experiential knowledge of the problem is key. Such peers have moved beyond the distortions of popular folklore ("beer isn't as bad as hard liquor") and yet still retain the immediacy of those "who have been there."

Now suppose that your neighbors are trusted friends and peers, and in the course of the visit tell you how they used a county-sponsored program called Meals on Wheels when they were both recovering from a severe case of the flu. They explain how it worked, whom to call, and what to do to get started. Now how likely is it that you would avail yourself of the services provided by the agency? Recent research indicates that informal caregiver networks are a major factor "in defining the nature of problems, providing help, influencing what sources of outside help will be obtained, and aiding in adjustment to a wide range of acute and chronic problems. . . . Informal helping networks are well suited for providing concrete advice, emotional reassurances, an immediate response, long-term caring, and everyday assistance."[2]

It may be important to call the function of building and maintaining natural helping networks by the simple word "neighboring." Certainly one of the fundamental bases for being a good person and building a good society is the ancient Judeo-Christian command to love one's neighbor (Lev. 19:18, Mark 12:31).

Think for a moment about your own neighborhood—be it a high-rise apartment, suburban development, central city housing cluster, or far-flung rural countryside. In whose hands is the care of that neighborhood? Who is going to care about those qualities of people and place that make a neighborhood a decent, habitable, happy, and healthy place to live? Building superintendents, government workers, elected officials, and social service personnel are all partial answers. The most important answer, however, is the resident, the citizen, the neighbor.

Many people would like to be good neighbors, but our society no longer takes this task very seriously. Neighborly service and compassion have increasingly become the province of professionals—clergy, social workers, city workers, therapists, and the like. The situation is not conducive to the building of good neighborhoods or good neighbors. Dependence on the experts leaves residents feeling powerless and does nothing to build better communities. It narrows the scope of public life and leaves the individual feeling alone and impotent in the face of institutions and bureaucracies too large to comprehend and too distant for contact. Moreover, our society has not recognized that the fundamental response to evil, the most basic actions in the restoration of the good, are rooted in the act of being neighborly.

New York Times reporter Daniel Goleman probed the matter in his account of a study being conducted to research the lives of those non-Jews in Europe who risked their existence during World War II to aid Jews in surviving the Nazi terror. The intent of the research program was to find the common threads in the lives of those few who offered help to their Jewish neighbors, and to see how they differ from those who might have helped but didn't. From interviews with over 140 rescuers and from other research, the project leaders have begun to focus their attention on formative influences within the family and neighborhood. Parents encouraged altruism when they firmly but warmly guided their children to be helpful and to share with their friends. However, as one of the researchers, Dr. Ervin Staub, a psychologist at the University of Massachusetts states, "Goodness, like evil, often begins in small steps. Heroes evolve; they aren't born. Very often the rescuers made only a small commitment at the start—to hide someone for a day or two. But once they had taken that step, they began to see themselves differently, as someone who helps. What starts as mere willingness becomes intense involvement."[3]

Arthur Morgan, former director of the Tennessee Valley Authority, and founder of Community Service, Inc., wrote:

For the preservation and transmission of the fundamentals of civilization, vigorous wholesome community life is imperative. Unless many people live and work in the intimate relationships of community life, there can never emerge a truly unified nation, or a community of mankind. If I do not love my neighbor whom I know, how can I love the human race, which is but an abstraction? If I have not learned how to work with a few people, how can I be effective with many?[4]

In the absence of this concrete, practical, day-to-day experience, being neighborly has become a sentimental symbol for a generalized attitude toward the world in general and no one in particular. Arthur Morgan is right, there is no better place to learn love of neighbor than one's actual neighborhood. There is the place to center the work of weaving goodness into our souls and into the fabric of society.

Neighborhoods are held together, made hospitable and safe, by their internal relationships. Such relationships grow out of the communal sharing of friendships, common values, and experiences that occur while shopping, looking for a lost pet, shoveling snow off sidewalks, relating to schools, and on and on. Some neighborhoods have a strong social fabric that is made up of these elements and relationships. Often, however, our local communities have a very weak social fabric, indeed so weak that it is not able to function as a support net or moralnet for the families and individuals who live in that community, as the following examples show:

1. One school administrator laments the lack of a strong social fabric in his affluent suburb in the Midwest. "There is no community in this area. Sure, we have agency collaboration and networks of cooperation between the school system and social service agencies but at the neighborhood level—at the level of scouts, sports, clubs, citizens' associations—we just don't have community. The elementary school PTA and the neighborhood swim club probably do more to bring some cohesion to the community than anything else. As a school system we have to build walls to keep churches at some distance because of our pluralistic society. Strengthening a neighborhood's community cohesion is something the ordinary citizen has to do—what the churches call lay people."

2. In another part of the country a group of older people, sixtyish and up, met for several weeks to identify the needs of the elderly in their rural county and examine the role of the churches in meeting those needs. They discovered that numerous service programs were available, some sponsored by government agencies, some by churches, and others by social organizations. But the committee also found that a gap existed between the needs and the willingness of the elderly to make use of existing services. The committee found that the wide array of services was almost universally regarded as being for those who are no longer capable— older people who must, for health or financial reasons, give

up their independence. Older people prefer to rely on their natural helping network of family, friends, and neighbors for the support and help they need. The problem is that in many cases this network is now weak or missing, and so the elderly try to tough it out alone before giving up.

3. A Protestant laywoman spends all summer organizing her large suburban congregation into local area "shepherd's groups." She wants the families in the "community of strangers" to experience the type of support and interaction among families and neighbors that were so important to her growing up as a child in a small southern town. Her pastor solicits all this volunteer energy because he hopes to build a greater sense of belonging within the congregation. But the neighborhood people who do not belong to the congregation see the effort as an attempt by the church to strengthen its own private internal cohesion and not as a service to the community.

4. A California community of mostly elderly residents organized a community safety patrol to combat the rising crime rate. Pairs of seasoned citizens roamed the neighborhood wearing bright yellow jackets and carrying walkie-talkie radios. A crime prevention researcher, noting the 48 percent decline in crime over a two-year period, comments that the crime rate "is the blood pressure of any neighborhood. When that neighborhood lacks cohesion, the crime rate goes up. When the neighborhood comes together, and when neighbors begin helping each other—though not as a nosy, everyone-in-everyone-else's business sort of way—the crime rate very quickly subsides."[5]

The need for neighboring may be triggered by something as ordinary as running out of eggs or needing a hammer. A snow storm, illness, the birth of a child, an accident, crime, zoning appeals, election campaigns, trying to locate a good plumber, organizing a Fourth of July festival, a car that won't start—these are the sort of major and minor crises that cause us to look to neighbors for help. Effective neighborhood contexts are those in which the larger number of persons can enter a rich, close-linked system of goodwill held together by the mutual help of friends and neighbors. In contrast, "help seeking which is initially too widely scattered or eventually too reliant on formal or professional helpers" is less effective in reducing stress and helping people to pursue life change and life development goals.[6]

One researcher lists the normal functions of natural helping networks as: (1) providing emotional support; (2) providing specific information; (3) filling in when close relationships are broken by death, illness, divorce, or separation (or when an additional helping hand is needed because close relationships do not suffice); (4) linking people to good professional help; and (5) serving instead of professionals when professionals are not trusted or not available.[7]

A sixth function might be added to this list: The moral-net function of serving to help individuals reorder their world of value and meaning when it has been broken by events or transitions. Many of the changes in our lives can cause us to fundamentally reexamine the moral order we have established for ourselves, the system of values and schemes of interpretation through which we assign significance to our life and activity. One acquaintance has described the loss of personal significance she felt when, after years of medical investigation and three miscarriages, she finally realized that she was not going to be a natural mother. That which she had looked to for meaning and as a central value orientation was not to be. Functioning as a moralnet, natural helpers offer validation and confirmation to those who are searching for meaning. Sometimes we need more than casual, customary social support; we need moral and spiritual support to help us knit together a life structure that is grounded in our deepest values and most treasured hopes.

In addition to these specific helping functions, neighboring involves some less visible activities that continually serve to mend and strengthen the social fabric of the community. Simple day-to-day conversation and observation of others and their patterns of living create shared norms and values. These interactions can form the stable backdrop to daily living, bringing a sense of harmony and security to living. Just seeing Mr. Smith, eighty and arthritic, set out early each morning for his brisk walk to the convenience store for coffee and doughnuts is a small daily symbol of the strength of the human spirit. Sights and scenes like this provide stability and richness to the community and hence strengthen the good-people system.

In the past we could expect that such helping relationships and community activities would simply happen spontaneously in the normal course of living. In many communities and neighborhoods this is no longer so. Indeed it can be argued that a large number of civic policies, institutional practices, and social programs have actually contributed to a weakening of neighborhood cohesion, and hence to a greater dependence on the intervention of professionals and outside agencies with a consequent increase in the gap between the help such agencies can offer and the general public they would serve. In such a situation the individual citizen must take the initiative to overcome this gap and to increase community cohesion. Fortunately, it can and is being done.

The proliferation in the number, variety, and effectiveness of mutual help or self-help support systems and groups is a dramatic example of the yearning and ability people have to give and receive help on a peer basis. "Central to a self-help group is the idea of sharing feelings, perceptions and problems with others who have had the same experience. The group can pass on very practical advice to new members, such as what life is like after a mastectomy or how to cope with the birthday of a child who has died."[8]

Dr. Frank Riessman, director of the National Self-Help Clearing House, estimates that 15 million Americans are involved in 500,000 such groups. Some examples of groups begun to serve the needs of just one category, the elderly, are the Alzheimer's Disease and Related Disorders Association, Parkinsonian societies, stroke clubs, family support groups for families where care is being given frail elderly, and widowed persons groups. The list of mutual help groups and associations is almost endless. Almost all focus on the experiential knowledge and social support of individual men and women who share a common problem. The initiation of self-help groups seems to require no more than two people who share pain from a similar cause.

Some years ago a couple in their early twenties, freshly married and very much still in the throes of learning how to sort out the dilemmas of family life, had their first son born in the rough and ready atmosphere of a U.S. Naval hospital. They took him home armed with very little guidance in infant care and with an enormous sense of the sudden overwhelming responsibility that was theirs. After only a few days at home they noticed that his tiny hands and feet were raw, to the point of leaving bloody trails on the sheets of his crib. Their first reaction was to suppose that this was the result of the harsh linen that had been used at the hospital. After a few more days passed and the situation had not improved, they realized that something was wrong. Thus began a series of visits to a succession of doctors. Finally the diagnosis was delivered. The infant had a very rare and potentially life-threatening skin disorder called epidermolysis bullosa. Though little information was available, the doctors could say that several levels of severity were possible, that the outer layers of his skin would slough off, leaving his hands and feet, at the least, raw and exposed. There was and is no cure, and very little was known about any form of treatment. As young, brand-new parents, they were confronted by a situation in which the

experts knew almost nothing and around which their anx-
ieties were enormous. There did not seem to be any place
to turn to get help. Fortunately, their worst fears were not
realized and the boy's condition turned out to be the mild-
est form of the disease. Looking back they can now see that
they were passive consumers of the medical help available
and simply accepted the ignorance of the medical profession. That was a mistake. In recent years they have watched
the dramatic growth of a national self-help association for
epidermolysis bullosa sufferers and their families. It shares
information and has lobbied to foster major new research
into the disease. It provides contacts with others who have
the same fears and problems to face in the day-to-day experience with their children. All this help and effort now
exists because of the initiative, vision, and leadership of one
mother of one child. She was not willing to be a passive
consumer, and so she set about finding and bringing into
concert the energy of the many parents who shared this
common experience. This story has been repeated time and
time again.

Parents Anonymous is a mutual aid group for parents
who have been involved in child abuse. Over 75 percent of
such parents were themselves abused as children. The groups
meet on a regular basis to help the parents air their feelings
in a nonjudgmental setting and to work at nonabusive ways
of responding to the stresses of the parental role. How did
Parents Anonymous begin?

In 1969, a distraught young mother appeared at a child guidance
clinic in Southern California and asked for help. She said she was
scared about the way she was abusing her daughter. During the
previous three years she had sought "cures" from nine other
agencies, but nothing had worked. When the intaker worker informed her that there was a six-month waiting list for treatment
at the clinic, the young mother went to pieces and began pound-
ing on the desk.

"I need help NOW!" she shouted. "My daughter will be dead

in six months, and you'll be more responsible than me because you're rational and I'm not!"

The alarmed clinic worker picked up the phone and made two calls: one to a psychiatric social worker to evaluate the woman for entry into the state mental hospital, the other to child protective services to intervene on behalf of the mother's children.[9]

This mother and the social worker sent to evaluate her founded Parent's Anonymous as a kitchen-table support group. There are now more than 1,200 chapters in forty-five states.

At the turn of this century financing a new home was an arduous process. One could purchase a building lot from a developer on an installment plan, but only when the lot was paid off could one obtain a building loan from the banks. Such loans were usually short term, three to five years. The results of this economic system were that the burgeoning suburbs developed in economic segregation, with many groups effectively excluded from the housing market. To meet this problem, trade and craft groups, church groups, and ethnic groups began to form small, locally controlled corporations that pooled the savings of the member shareholders. These funds were then loaned to the members, sometimes chosen by lottery, so that they could build a home. It is from these small community associations that today's savings and loan associations have evolved.[10]

When help is too far removed from the need, or when professionals are given responsibility for what ordinary people can do better, because they add a little of themselves to the offering, or when large institutions treat segments of the population as clients rather than creative contributors, or when people get fed up because services they need are not forthcoming, they do what comes naturally—they band together and get what they want. It has always been so and it is today.

John Naisbitt cites the amazing growth in homeowner

and condo associations as evidence of the demand for neighbors that are effectively run by community participation. He reports that there were 35,000 such groups in 1980 and that the number had grown to almost 65,000 by 1985. "With neighborhood groups sprouting, and gaining in professionalism, political action increasingly will take place at the local level. That's where tough issues, like crime and education problems, will be tackled, in tune with [the] trend toward decentralization."[11]

Far more than any of us realize the tools for the transformation and repair of our society rest in our own hands (see Figure 6). Four conditions must be met if people are to be motivated to actually make change. Examine these conditions in your own life and situation. If all four are present or can be brought into being then you will be ready to act.

1. *You must be dissatisfied with the status quo.* There must be some level of experienced pain, discomfort, or unrest resulting from the present state of affairs. Instead of denying or repressing it, enter into the specific anxiety and hurt

Figure 6. Taking Responsibility: Being the Author of Your Own Story

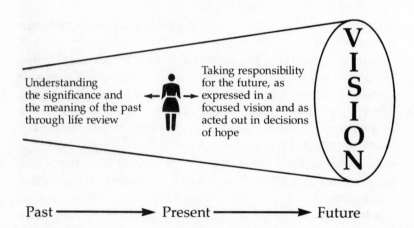

Understanding the significance and the meaning of the past through life review

Taking responsibility for the future, as expressed in a focused vision and as acted out in decisions of hope

VISION

Past ⟶ Present ⟶ Future

of your concrete situation. Biblical scholar Walter Brueg-
gemann states that "the great moments in biblical faith
characteristically happen when somebody has the courage
to act out the cry or the defiance to say 'it isn't working.' "[12]

What is not working in your life? Is there a specific
person or hurt that preoccupies you, where you long to see
help rendered and conditions changed? We all have the tendency to make ourselves feel better by assigning the responsibility for our situation to someone else. Psychologist
Scott Peck calls this "casting our pain on society."[13]

The first step out of apathy and into responsibility is to
claim the pain and to openly acknowledge the hurting places
among us. Saying it is not right, that it is not working, is
a public affirmation that opens the door to hope.

2. *You must have a clear and promising future vision—a
bright, well-stated, compelling statement of the future you hope
to create.* Taking action means that to some degree you are
going to become a leader. You must begin to enroll others
in meeting the problem, and you must have an internal
guide for your own actions. You must create a picture that
you can communicate to others of the positive future you
intend to build. Your vision will be grounded in your faith
and values, but its language and its images will be those of
the situation you are trying to address. Vague pieties and
broad generalities will not do. The vision needs to speak
to the concrete realities discovered in the longing of your
unrest. It should be expressed not as a negation of that pain
but as the positive achievement of a new, good, and transformed situation. Dennis Geaney, in an article entitled "What
Must I Be to Minister?," says that the person who offers
to a community "vision, caring or leadership is often described as such in street language, not with the title 'minister.' In any group of people, there are usually one or more
people who are recognized by the group as having some
kinship or access to the divine through their caring or
wisdom that helps all see life in a larger perspective than

the immediate concern and thus lifts up the human experience, eliciting faith, hope and love."[14] A vision is a statement of hope made concrete in the language, images, and metaphors of the street, of the place where the action is and will be.

3. *You must be aware of or know about one or two feasible and tangible first steps to take on the path toward the vision.* Every journey begins with a single step, and that step is often the hardest. Experience suggests that the most important possible first step is to find one other person who shares or can be brought to share the vision. Pat Charles, an experienced community organizer, says: "Of course there will be resistance and apathy—never mind the people who say you can't do it—just look for one person who sees the vision with you and you've found all you need." People tend to greet this advice with skepticism. They usually want to form a committee or write a foundation proposal or seek the backing of some major institution. Don't be misled by such erroneous folk wisdom. Finding one other trusted colleague who is ready to take responsibility for the vision is essential. Together you can look at your strengths and assess what is happening in the community so that you can be guided to your subsequent steps on the basis of sound knowledge and an informed intuition. No matter how good the plan, this is a very complicated and ever-changing world. Perhaps you will never really be clear about anything more than your vision and the one or two immediate next steps. All the rest will often seem completely unknown and full of risk and uncertainty.

4. *If you are not yet ready to move it is either because the three conditions above have not been met, or because they have not been dealt with in sufficient strength to outweigh the costs, real or imagined, of taking action.* Can you identify the costs? Do they seem to be financial or moral or emotional? Taking action will be costly. Every change from the status quo requires giving something up or taking on something more, and sometimes both. The costs will always be real.

There are some important things you can do to respond to the costs. One of the easiest is to increase the strength of your convoy of support by filling in the gaps in your personal network of social support. Who are the people you rely on to provide affection, affirmation, aid, and comfort? Based on the image of the naval convoy of World War II, psychologist Robert Kahn developed the concept of a convoy of social support to give the picture of those who accompany us on our life journey in the exchange of help and security. The convoy metaphor helps us to recognize that as the course of our life changes, other people will move in and out of our escort of social support. Our own position and role in the convoy will change over time. Every major new undertaking, every new turn in direction, alters the relationships and provides an opportunity for us to carefully consider those who surround us, whether their position is near or far. The responsibility to stay in relationship and in communication with the members of your convoy is yours and yours alone. The number of those you count as escorts and support companions will change as they, in turn, make course changes in their own lives. You may well be called upon to search out and add new members to your convoy.

Some time ago a friend told me that he and his wife had few friends they could depend on, and he wondered if it was the nature of the community in which they lived. Over the years I have noticed that this couple seldom signal for help. Very little is done to keep us informed of the major events in their family. Keeping on station with them takes repeated effort, which is seldom reciprocated. The evidence suggests that they may be among that large group of folk who consider it the responsibility of the community or the church or the synagogue or someone else to provide the fleet of helpers they need to get through the storms and perils of life. Such people are bound to be disappointed. Just as no community or organization can take from us the responsibility of steering our own course, neither can they assume our obligation to find those who will be by our side on that journey.

If the cost seems too great to act on your vision, you can go into the wilderness and pray. A recent day-long session of an executive development program sponsored by a major university had for its topic career planning and development. There were over forty participants, men and women in their late thirties and early forties. The lecturer emphasized to the group that this program was "quality off-line time," an opportunity to step back from the pressures of the job and really consider where they wanted to go with their careers.

As a first step participants were asked to carefully examine their (1) values and life goals, (2) core skills and competencies, and (3) personal and interpersonal styles. His point was that these fundamental aspects of who we are can only be taken out and examined on special occasions. He was trying to help the participants use their time out to gain inner perspective on their active career and work lives. His advice was a modern version of an ancient truth. The more one hopes to engage life with integrity and courage, the more necessary it is to draw apart in solitude, to drop the reins of daily activity and let the depths of one's soul gently emerge. Tilden Edwards suggests that one of the foundations of spiritual discipline is the rhythm of movement between gentle reception and active, generative productivity. He calls on us to learn a disciplined oscillation "between active doing (ministry) time and receptive being (sabbath) time."[15] The sabbath experience of attentively resting in the Lord is not easily mixed with the structured demands, unrelenting expectations, and technical jargon that tend to dominate our arenas of active, purposeful endeavor. When the two are simply mixed together the result is usually noisy confusion that is neither active ministry nor sabbath receptivity. Many organized experiences directed at ministry are full of static because there are too many people involved who are looking to that experience as a means of spiritual discernment and development. Many of the experiences of Sunday morning are confused and unsatisfying, because they occur "online" and are frenzied, highly organized pressure points for all concerned. Learning to harmonize the active-receptive rhythm is a true discipline.

Scripture, prayer, meditation, and spiritual direction have been the ancient guides for the quiet journey of receptivity, for the times when we rest in the Lord. They can be guides, of course, only when they are familiar and trusted rather than objects of suspicion and awkward unfamiliarity. The more crucial and costly a change, the more difficult it may be to put things into their proper perspective. As countless workers have found, the lure of a prestigious job and of a large salary can make it extremely difficult to keep in perspective life goals of community service and strong family ties.

It is possible for every individual, young or old, rich or poor, to make a fundamental and substantive contribution to the good of society. One of the dangers of the ministry of the laity is that it can be seen as an enthusiasm, as another activity to be added, through the best of intentions, to a life already crowded and overwhelmed by a multitude of conflicting concerns and competing demands. To keep life in perspective, carefully tend the relationships, and hold to a focused vision of the good may indeed be costly by many standards. But the question of cost needs to be addressed. The retreat into solitude is a return to the ground of our being where we can listen for the truths we hold most dear. Author Frederick Buechner has focused much of his writing on the stories of his own life. He suggests that "we must learn to listen to the cock-crows and hammering and tick-tock of our lives for the holy and elusive word that is spoken to us out of their depths."[16] Your vision is the statement of meaning you hope to see embedded in your life. No one finds it easy to cut through the clutter of life with clear vision and unwavering determination. Taking time out to get our bearings is essential. One of the major roles of the gathered church is to help us learn how to use Scripture, prayer, meditation, and spiritual direction as compass guides to that place of rest where we touch our most essential nature. Whether we use these guides when our life is about to take a major turn is up to us.

The worth of any endeavor has two price tags. One is the cost placed upon it by the market forces of society, the other is the price you are willing to pay.

THE GAP BETWEEN PERSONAL LIVING AND PUBLIC ENDEAVOR

As we have discovered, the line between personal, private matters and public affairs is seriously out of kilter. To distinguish between our private and our public lives should seem simple, and yet it is not. To balance what we do on the record—publicly—and what we do off the record—privately—should seem easy, but it is not. Much of what we regard as public, our work life or our church life, is likely to occur completely off the public record and leave little impact. Life inside any of our major corporate entities—industrial, religious, or educational—can be surprisingly private in nature. Meetings are closed to the public, the proceedings restricted to those who belong, the subject matter confined to issues of an in-house nature. Insofar as the public good is concerned, the individual is left with nothing more than the pious hope that the business of the corporation will contribute to the good of society as a whole. Critical theorist Jurgen Habermas speaks of the tendency to civic privatism, "that is, political abstinence combined with an orientation to career, leisure, and consumption."[17] Civic privatism takes the political and public order for granted in the expectation that the system will provide the personal rewards of money, leisure time, and security.

Our private lives are in a similar state of confusion. Those realms of life and activity that are purely our own personal spheres of endeavor may indeed be more involved in the affairs of the public state than we imagine. As George Will reminds us, we consider one individual regularly getting drunk on his way home from work a personal and private matter. On the other hand, when the same private behavior becomes characteristic of millions, then we recognize a public crisis—which leads to changes in the drinking and licensing laws, as has happened in England and Sweden.[18]

In Sweden there is an interesting attitude toward what is public and what is private. An American walking along the shore of one of those sparkling Scandinavian lakes would notice, tucked back in the evergreen forests that line the stony banks, scores of small vacation cottages and cabins. Each cottage bears signs of individual ownership, there are many samples of the weekend craftsmanship of the proud owners. And yet the trail seems to lead right through the property attached to the cabin. This might make any foreign visitor nervous, especially one who came from Texas ranch country, where experience teaches that no one sets foot on another person's land without permission. In Sweden these cottages do stand on private land, but the right of privacy extends only a few feet from the door. The public has a right to use all the rest. It is a kind of common, and the public is also expected to exercise responsible stewardship.

Our major shopping malls are jam-packed on public holidays with crowds of shoppers. Going to the mall has become an urban pastime. The stroll down Main Street has been replaced by a stroll through the corridors of a complex of buildings. These malls are usually owned by some faceless corporation whose only motive is profit. And yet they are designed—and certainly not by accident—to give us the feel of enjoying the free, communal rights of citizens strolling the public streets or on the common.

The line between public and private is hard to draw and not easy to know. Where is the voice of the people really heard? Where does the public domain begin and end? We do know that, without the personal experience of open, recognized communal discourse and interchange, the legitimacy of public order will erode.

Free, civic, holiday festivals are getting scarce, but perhaps you can find a community where Memorial Day, Fourth of July, or Thanksgiving is still a shared, conspicuous, well-planned, neighborly public event. Perhaps you will need to revisit your own memories to find such an occasion. In any case, take note of what really happens at such public festivals.

First, it is a meeting of friends, neighbors, and strangers. People of all varieties mingle together with a genuine sense of hospitality and without threat or fear. You may meet someone you have not seen in years and stop to renew acquaintances. Perfect strangers will start sharing reactions and discussing the experience. The usual categories into which we classify people don't seem to matter here.

Second, if it is a real public festival and not some artificial, contrived, commercial imitation, there will be a great profusion of groups and organizations all mixed into the pot—performing, helping, cooking, guiding, selling, parading, singing. Service clubs, churches, Scouts, booster clubs, school bands, the hospital auxiliary, volunteer fire companies, and many more will have pitched in to entertain, feed, and otherwise help the festival happen. You will find all these groups and organizations working to a common end and in a spirit of fun and cooperation.

Third, the day has variety, texture, and color that lend drama and spirit impossible to achieve by other means. One can, of course, spend a lot of money and travel to large entertainment parks like Disney World and see something spirited and colorful. But it won't be the same, and it won't be as good, and for our society, not nearly so good.

Fourth, most of the fun, all the conviviality, and the drama will be free. The college president, the doctor, the plumber, the construction laborer, the school teacher, the farmer, the social workers, the lawyer, and the storekeeper are on the same level. Access is the same for all, no questions asked.

Fifth, a sense of common duties and responsibilities will prevail. It may show itself in the orderly manner the crowd moves from place to place or handles instructions from the festival directors. It may be nothing more than that people put their trash in receptacles and not on the street, but even that is quite a lot. What is being demonstrated, perhaps in a crowd of many thousands, is the sense of responsibility on the part of each individual for the good of the whole. The importance of such public civility is never clearer than in its absence. On May 30, 1985, riots at the European Champion's Cup soccer final in Brussels left thirty-eight dead and hundreds injured. Those savage events were part of an escalating pattern of violence at matches all over the world. At these events guard dogs, moats, electrified fences, and hordes of security police are beginning to replace the personal inner discipline to self-control and concern for the welfare of others that is the fundamental basis of public life. A simple first step toward such public violence is the attitude that says I paid my money; public safety, disposal of the trash and debris are someone else's responsibility.

What one sees in a good public festival are injections of hospitality, cooperation, drama, accessibility, and a sense of shared duty into the lifestream of our society. They show us how much we need these elements in public life if we are to foster good living. They also show us, by contrast, how little such real integration between personal endeavor and public affairs exists in American life today. As Amitai Etzioni reminds us, character development is "achieved by tying biological satisfaction to socially-acceptable gratifications (sublimation if you wish); by relating satisfaction to sensitivity to others, the psychic basis of mutuality; and by building ego-restraints, the basis of playing by the rules, and ego-involvement in the transcending (public) realm and issues, the basis of civility."[19]

If there are too many gaps between personal lives and public living, then sensitivity to others, playing by the rules, and responsible involvement in commonweal activities cannot be learned and become increasingly rare. As most often conceived, practiced, and promoted, ministry of the laity is little more than the private ministry of Christian folk. It has all too frequently been seen as Christians doing their unique thing, which society as a whole just does not yet appreciate. In every discussion of ministry in the workplace a frequent question is, "What is distinctively Christian about that?" The implication is that the validity of the ministry rests on its being an activity that is somehow peculiarly Christian in nature rather than on its contribution to the public good. The question defines ministry as what people do in the name of the church and continues the error of regarding the church's role in society as essentially that of a special interest lobby. A society that is simply a battleground for a thousand special interest groups will kill mutuality and civility. This is, of course, a reflection of the corporate culture of the church, which functionally defines ambassadorship for Christ as being a lobbyist for the Christian enterprise.

In truth, ambassadorship for Christ is service on behalf of all who are in need, a public ministry for the good of the world. Such ministry is public to the degree it genuinely integrates personal endeavors with the public good. Family activities can in this sense be quite public and activities in the office quite private.

Ministry of the laity is a state of mind and heart in which what one does is consciously and intentionally neighborly in character. It requires inner strength, courage to persevere, hope invested in a vision not yet realized, and the perspective to question and challenge accepted practice, to sustain this ministry; and these are gifts of grace. Nothing in the Judeo-Christian heritage suggests that these are gifts to satisfy the personal quest for fulfillment, even if that end is disguised by calling it salvation. As Frederick Buechner says, "To journey for the sake of saving our own lives is little by little to cease to live in any sense that really matters, even to ourselves, because it is only by journeying for the world's sake—even when the world bores and sickens and scares you half to death—that little by little we start to come alive."[20]

In his book *Statecraft as Soulcraft*, George Will advances the view that all public enterprise is a grappling with the question "What kind of people do we expect our citizens to be?" He defines statecraft or statesmanlike practices as the care of our time, the cultivation of good character through "locating the region of probable success in bringing citizens through law to worthy lives."[21]

Substitute for "law" the term "public practices," and you have a good definition of ministry of the laity. Will describes the confusion and ambivalence present in the realm of civics and politics over the development of the sentiments, manners, and public opinion of the citizenry. There is a similar ambivalence in the realm of theological polity, and that has serious consequences for the civic illiteracy of our citizens. Our forebears separated church and state and thus ruled out of bounds the theocratic solution to the question of how ought we to live. If the public arena is defined by issues such as a shared political philosophy, neighborliness, the legitimation of the basic rules that govern a good society, then both church and state have been uncertain about how to enter this arena and have vacillated between leaving it entirely alone or inappropriately attempting to control it. It regards love of God and love of neighbor as completely inseparable. It places the responsibility for the public arena squarely on the shoulders of each individual citizen. It sees that both church and state, indeed all our public institutions, have the responsibility to consciously invest the citizenry with their public responsibility. Ministry of the laity calls upon the church as an institution to give its attention to helping its members learn the spiritual disciplines that will sustain an active engagement with the world. Ministry of the laity is a vision of a church whose culture and practices help its members:

- see the choices they face in their daily lives
- discern God's will for those choices
- ask God for the courage to act
- learn through the consequences what new choices invite them to "prove what is the will of God" for their lives. [22]

Epilogue

Ministry of the laity, as we have defined it, is the outward, active, expressive life and activity of people who regard themselves as belonging to the people of God. This ministry is largely carried out in the pluralistic modern world, which is a non-Christian context. It is a world created good but wrecked by evil. It is a world that can be, and is even now being, transformed and repaired by God.

As Christians, we assume that our task of ministry—the giving of the activity of our total lives in discipleship—unites us as coworkers with God in this effort. We further assume that the energy, the courage, the heart to engage in this ministry comes from an active, living relationship with God through the Holy Spirit. We know that our ministry is deeply flawed—that the expression of our lives can be and often is sinful, careless, and not good. We sometimes destroy what we intend to build up. Thus our ministry is acted out in the tension between the appropriation of God's forgiveness and God's commandment that we love our neighbors as ourselves.

We believe that being thoughtful, reflective, and intentional will improve the quality of our ministry. We also look to the institution of the church to be a source of guidance in threading our way through the maze of modern life and more importantly to provide settings of retreat and worship where we can be renewed and sustained in the task of ministry. The local congregation has the opportunity to help its members move appropriately from the inward spiritual encounter with God's power and love to the outward expression of that love in the turmoil of society.

Ministry of the laity requires good people—whole people—people living out their lives with meaning and personal fulfillment and helping others do the same. Although we cannot define goodness, we can talk about it, and we can know when it is present and when it is not.

Goodness basically has to do with individuals, the values they hold, and whether their actions are loyal to those values. But good individuals have relationships with other people and can impart their values and behaviors to their common life. So goodness is related to people in community, expanding to interact with the institutions that serve them and the environment that sustains them. The good, then, is personal, corporate, and contextual. It is also spiritual. To explore and understand it we must call on the best knowledge and insights of psychology, sociology, the natural sciences, theology, and philosophy.

Experience teaches that good people produce good families and good communities, a good nation, and a good world; and in turn good communities and good families, and a good world, and a good nation produce good people. While hope of perfection in society denies the human predicament, the failure to hope and work for perfection assumes that the imperfect present order is a given—God-given—and that a better world and better people are not possible.

A daughter, Pam, is born to John and Sally. As she grows and matures into adolescence and adulthood, the influences on her life are many—parents, siblings, relatives, peers, friends, teachers, competitors, coworkers, sales clerks, receptionists, nurses, doctors, the police, mail carriers, strangers, people with disabilities, waiters and waitresses, best friends, boyfriends, actors and actresses, thieves, clergy, and many more. Pam's life is formed in relationship to day-care centers, schools, clubs, churches, governments, political organizations, informal cliques, shopping malls, libraries, parks, recreation centers, and hospitals. Influences include the nature and quality of life in the neighborhoods, cities or counties, state, and nation in which she resides. Included are racial and ethnic diversity, social status, wealth, employment opportunities, ecology, climate, lifestyles, and value systems.

Pam's life is, of course, shaped in great degree also according to personal attributes that are given—her race, physical attractiveness, health, intelligence, social class, and personality characteristics. The complexity and relationship of forces that form Pam and the patterns of her life are of course beyond comprehension. But this intricate combination of hereditary and environmental forces, together with the way Pam receives, assimilates, and acts on the full range of stimuli that envelop her, will give the world Pam—Pam as she actually turns out to be and to live.

But that is not the end of the story. Pam will exert some kind of influence on all the people with whom she will interact, those she will know, or know of, or be known by. Each of these lives will be different in some degree because of her thoughts, values, or actions. She will shape institutions, processes, values, and the quality of life in the communities where she lives and through them the nation and the world.

In the ideal world, the culture of the society into which Pam is born leads her to become a good person. And Pam participates as part of the society in revisioning and renewing the society so that it remains good. The system of good people and good societies participating together in mutually shaping interaction tends to break down when the social order changes and when forces of social life combine to produce fewer good people and people who are less good. The system may break down also if citizens lose their vision of the good and their perspective regarding their essential role in the continued renewal of the good society. It is not possible to know exactly what goes wrong or when the downward cycle starts. Since by definition people and societies include one another in their very beings, it is impossible to lay blame. What is certain is that people—individually and together—have a choice: They can let their common life deteriorate, or they can nurture and build good communities and a good world.

Even if most communities in America today were valued and valuing settings for shaping good people, we would need to address this problem. The need for rethinking the kind of life we want and repairing and rebuilding our social structures and processes to make it real is ever present. And of course the state of repair or disrepair of a person, a building, or a society is always one of degree. It is unmistakably plain that modern America's social ordering of its people does not contribute effectively to the development of good people, that communal structures are fragmented and competitive, and that radical rebuilding is essential. Ordinary good people, laypeople, can accomplish this rebuilding. People, not institutions or professional bureaucracies, are the only ones who can.

The field of health offers a good example of what is possible. No area of our lives has been more professionalized than health care, but this is fast changing. At a recent meeting of three hundred health care professionals, Tom Ferguson, physician and editor of the magazine *Medical Self-Care*, discussed trends in the health care system. "We're going through a profound change in our health-care system. . . . We're on the crest of a powerful, historic wave."

He predicts that by the end of this century,

there's not going to be a primary practitioner. The doctor is not going to be the glue that puts the health-care system together. The individual is going to be the glue.

We're moving from a profession-oriented to a layperson-oriented system.[1]

Another recent news report told of the reduced risk of heart disease in the United States. Healthier lifestyles were given credit for "more than half of the dramatic fall over the past two decades in the risk of dying from coronary artery disease." Dr. Lee Goldman was quoted as saying that "the major message to the average American is that you can do more for your own risk of dying from heart disease than your doctor can do for you. . . . doctors can give advice but the average person has a lot of control over his own destiny here."[2]

Martin Marty picked up a good-people story from *Mennonite Banner*.

The most popular handbook for village workers in the Third World is probably *Where There Is No Doctor*, a guide for treating countless wounds and diseases. The book has been translated into twenty-nine languages. A worker of the Mennonite Central Committee was surprised to discover that David Werner, author of the book, is not a medical doctor but a biologist who went to Mexico twenty years ago to study and draw birds, trees, and flowers. In a recent interview with the Mennonite worker, Werner told how he first conceived the idea to write the book: "It was while he slept in a hospital shack of mountain-dwellers who had three sick children. Werner realized that although he was not a physician, he did have access to information that could help the children. From that time on he began collecting medical supplies and text books. Finally he wrote his book." [Marty's comment is that Werner] may have contributed more to human good than anything publicized at Humana [Hospital].[3]

Somehow when people catch a vision of what needs to be done and figure out how and where to begin, each step seems to lead them to the next one. The result is that people take responsibility for their own lives. When that happens they seem to be better cared for than when professionals do it for them.

If there is one overriding issue in the world today that crosses all national boundaries and evokes fear and even despair in the hearts of people of all classes and political persuasions, it is the threat of nuclear holocaust. News reports on the anniversaries of the bombings of Hiroshima and Nagasaki remind us of the horrors of mass destruction that occurred during World War II and the even greater threat of nuclear annihilation now.

Who are the professionals who will maintain the peace of the future? Who can assure us that the political leaders of the world who control massive arsenals of nuclear weapons have the will and the power to guarantee the safety of the world? As more nations get nuclear capabilities, the threat of unrestrained deployment and use increases. Periodic terrorist attacks in all parts of the globe, paralyzing even the strongest of political leaders, remind us that our world is far from safe.

Perhaps the real professionals in world peace are the rank-and-file laypeople in politics—those of us who have never studied political science or participated in political activities or weapons technology. It may be that the road to world peace runs through the family networks, the schools, the churches, the small communities of all nations where people learn to relate to other people in caring and benevolent ways and where the values of integrity in human relationships are established. It may be that good people building good communities and good societies will thereby establish a world in which people will require those who lead them politically to search and work for loving and just relationships for all the people of the world.

Our analysis is simple. We do not pretend to give a blueprint for enormously complex political and social relationships. We do question, however, how we can effectively deal with issues of world peace if we cannot deal with peace issues in the structures we inhabit. A community or society in which a significant part of the population has the ability to be semiliterate in basic values is, we believe, a community or a society that will be responsive to world issues and less likely to be passive in the face of threats to all of the people of the world.

Rebuilding communities is not going to cure all our ills. There will continue to be individual as well as bureaucratic problems to solve. However, the creation of caring and just environments for people and families who are struggling to survive or who only need the human touch in order to press on can again become the foundation of a just and sustainable world.

Neighbors and their institutions can mediate the needs and the solutions. The mediating system has only to do what it can do and that will be enough. Recognizing that our lives need to be perfected at the place where life matters most, where it is lived every day, we can see that the family and the neighborhood comprise the nerve center for the rest of the system of human relationships. If that is so, and if we laypeople act, we will get better communites *and* a better world. We will also get better people.

Notes

PREFACE

1. From book review of James W. Fowler's *Stages of Faith* by Craig Dykstra in *New Catholic World*, as reprinted in *Ministry and Mission* (Atlanta: Emory University, Candler School of Theology) 7, no. 3 and 4 (Summer/Fall 1981).

PROLOGUE

1. Benjamin Franklin, *The Autobiography of Ben Franklin* (New Haven: Yale University Press, 1964), 147.
2. Ibid., 156.
3. Quoted from a tape recording of John A. Coleman's address to a conference sponsored by the Office on the Ministry of the Laity of the U.S. Catholic Conference held at the University of Notre Dame, South Bend, Indiana, April 1984.
4. Robert McLean, quoted in "Responsibility to Write Theology," *Cathedral College of the Laity Newsletter* 4, no. 2 (June 1983): 1.
5. Hendrik Kraemer, *A Theology of the Laity* (Philadelphia: The Westminster Press, 1958).
6. Yves M. J. Congar, *Lay People in the Church: A Study for a Theology of the Laity*, translated by Donald Attwater (London: Bloomsbury Pub. Co., 1957).
7. October 1982 article by George Peck entitled, "World Baptists and the Ministry of the Laity," distributed as part of the Laos in Ministry information service of the Lutheran Church in America.
8. Undated article by Jean Hamilton entitled, "All My Best Friends are Ministers—and Some of Them Are Ordained," distributed as part of the 99%er information service of the Episcopal church.
9. *Challenge to the Laity*, edited by Russell Barta (Huntington, Indiana: Our Sunday Visitor, 1980), 24.
10. Kraemer, *Theology of the Laity*, 167.
11. Ibid.
12. Donald Smith, *Clergy in the Crossfire* (Philadelphia: Westminster Press, 1973). See also James D. Anderson, "Pastoral Support of Clergy—Role

Development Within Local Congregations," *Pastoral Psychology* XII, no. 212 (March 1971): 9–14; and Margaretta K. Bowers, *Conflicts of the Clergy: A Psychodynamic Study* (New York: Thomas Nelson and Sons, 1963).

13. Harvey Cox, "The 'New Breed' in American Churches: Sources of Social Activism in American Religion," *Daedalus* 96, no. 1 (Winter 1967).

14. An article entitled "Understanding Grows on Both Sides of the Clergy-Laity Gap," by Margaret Spur Gilman, distributed by Lay Ministries Committee, 15 pages.

15. Excerpt from a letter written in 1980.

16. Thomas C. Campbell, *The Fragmented Layman: An Empirical Study of Lay Attitudes* (Philadelphia: Pilgrim Press, 1970), 216.

17. Os Guinness, interviewed in *The Wittenburg Door* 73 (June–July 1983): 19–20.

18. Charles Y. Glock, Benjamin B. Ringer, and Earl R. Babbie, *To Comfort and to Challenge: A Dilemma of the Contemporary Church* (Berkeley: University of California Press, 1967).

19. Ibid., 215.

20. Article entitled "Religion, Prejudice, and Personality," in Merton P. Strommen, ed., *Research on Religious Development: A Comprehensive Handbook* (New York: Hawthorne Books, 1971). See also Campbell, *Fragmented Layman*, 223.

21. From a story recounted by Dr. Dozier in a sermon preached at the ordination of Jane Hart Holmes Dixon, Good Shepherd Church, Burke, Virginia, January 16, 1982.

22. *Circuit Rider* (April 1985): 9.

23. John R. Sherwood and John C. Wagner, *Sources and Shapes of Power*, Into Our Third Century Series, edited by Ezra Earl Jones (Nashville: Abingdon, 1981), 119.

24. Marciniak *et al.*, *Challenge to the Laity*, 9.

25. Lou Mitchell, quoted in "Responsibility to Write Theology," *Cathedral College of the Laity Newsletter* 4, no. 2 (June 1983): 1.

26. Verna J. Dozier and Celia A. Hahn, *The Authority of the Laity* (Washington, D.C.: The Alban Institute, 1982), 40.

27. Kraemer, *Theology of the Laity*, 161.

28. Excerpt from a letter written in 1980.

29. Chester Williams, "Publish or Perish," *Forward* (Nashville: The United Methodist Foundation for Evangelism) 6, issue 2 (March 1985): 1.

1. THE IGNORANCE OF GOOD AND EVIL

1. "The Faith of Children," an interview with Robert Coles, *Sojourners Magazine* 11, no. 5 (May 1982): 16.

2. For an important discussion of this concept of literacy and its relationship to values on a global scale see James W. Botkin, Mahdi Elmandjra, and Mircea Malitza, *No Limits To Learning: A Report to the Club of Rome* (Oxford: Pergamon Press, 1979).

3. Eldridge Cleaver, *Soul on Ice* (Dell Books, 1968), 16.

4. *New Yorker* "Talk of the Town" (May 23, 1977): 24–25.

5. Christopher Lasch, *The Culture of Narcissism* (New York: Norton, 1979).

6. These stages were suggested by a reading of David Tyack and Elisabeth Hansot, *Managers of Virtue: Public School Leadership in America, 1820–1980* (New York: Basic Books, 1982). Hansot and Tyack describe three stages of public school development. We believe these stages are more broadly characteristic of American society as a whole.

7. Alexis de Tocqueville, *Democracy in America*, quoted in Wilson Carey McWilliams, *The Idea of Fraternity in America* (Berkeley: University of California Press, 1973), 200.

8. Richard J. Mengolis, "For the Volunteers, Dousing Flames Is Only Part of the Job," *Smithsonian Magazine* 14, no. 8 (November 1983): 155.

9. McWilliams, *Idea of Fraternity*, 487.

10. Rebecca West, *The Real Night* (New York: Viking, 1985), quoted in "Beginning a Posthumous Career," a review by Paul Gray, *Time* (March 25, 1985): 75.

11. Alexis de Tocqueville, *Democracy in America*, quoted by Martin E. Marty in *Context* (Chicago: Claretian Publications) 16, no. 20 (November 15, 1984).

12. Woodrow Wilson, *The State* (New York: Heath, 1889), 633–677 quoted by McWilliams, *Idea of Fraternity*, 487.

13. Milton Kotler, *Neighborhood Government* (Indianapolis and New York: Bobbs-Merrill, 1969), 26.

14. Maxine Schnall, *Limits: A Search for New Values* (New York: Crown Publishers, 1982), quoted in a review in *Renewal* 1, no. 24 (June 21, 1982): 3.

15. John Naisbitt, *1984—The Year Ahead* (Washington: The Naisbitt Group, 1984), 9.

16. Jane Mayer, "Hollywood Is Hoping Nuclear Drama Isn't a Box Office Bomb," *The Wall Street Journal* (July 19, 1983): 1.

17. Norman Lear, "Traveling Hopefully in Long Term," *Leading Edge* V, no. 7 (December 17, 1984): 2.

18. We are indebted to the creative thought and work of Robert G. Johnston for insight into the processes through which media and the processes of attitude survey interact to make normative values and behavior that at first are the alternatives of only a few.

19. Daniel Yankelovich, *New Rules in American Life: Searching for Fulfillment in a World Turned Upside Down* (New York: Random House, 1981) excerpted in *Psychology Today* (April 1981): 50.

20. James McGregor Burns, *Leadership* (New York: Harper & Row, 1978), 425.

2. THE GOOD-PEOPLE SYSTEM

1. Margaret Atwood, *Two-Headed Poems* (New York: Simon and Schuster, 1978), 56.
2. Gerhard Von Rad, *Genesis* (Philadelphia: Westminster, 1961), 59.
3. Lawrence C. Becker, "The Neglect of Virtue," *Ethics* 85, no. 2 (January 1975): 113.
4. John Spencer, "The Problem of Goodness," 1973–74, 3. Unpublished paper.
5. Christopher Alexander, *The Timeless Way of Building* (New York: Oxford, 1979), 25.
6. Ibid., 41.
7. Stanley Hauerwas, *A Community of Character* (Notre Dame: University of Notre Dame Press, 1981), 125.
8. Peter Marin, "Living in Moral Pain," *Psychology Today* (November 1981): 74.
9. Wendell Berry, *Standing by Words* (San Francisco: North Point Press, 1983), 67.
10. Paul Lehman, *Ethics In a Christian Context* (New York: Harper & Row, 1963), 350.
11. Aldo Leopold, *Sand County Almanac* (San Francisco: Sierra Club, Ballentine Books, 1970), 238–239.
12. Amitai Etzioni, *An Immodest Agenda* (New York: McGraw-Hill, 1983), 50.
13. Ivan Boszormenyi-Nagy and Geraldine M. Spark, *Invisible Loyalties* (Hagerstown: Harper & Row, 1973), 139.
14. Leopold, *Sand County*, 262.
15. Barry Commoner, *The Closing Circle* (New York: Alfred A. Knopf, 1971), 163.
16. Garrett Hardin, "The Tragedy of the Commons," *Science* 162 (December 13, 1968).
17. George C. Homans, *English Villagers of the Thirteenth Century* (New York: Harper & Row, 1970), 382.
18. Ibid., 401.
19. Paul Valentine, "Lost in The City," *The Washington Post*, Monday, July 30, 1984.
20. Draper L. Kauffman, Jr., *Systems One: An Introduction to Systems Thinking* (Champlin, Minn.: Future Systems, Inc., 1980), 17.
21. Robert Theobald, *Action Linkage Newsletter* (June 1984).
22. Berry, *Standing by Words*, 123.
23. Ibid., 74.
24. David Bohm, *Wholeness and the Implicate Order* (London: Ark Paperbacks, 1983), 25.

25. Berry, *Standing by Words*, 44.

3. THE FAMILY AND GOOD PEOPLE

1. Jerome Kagan, *The Nature of the Child* (New York: Basic Books, 1984), 243.
2. Ibid., 244.
3. Walker Percy, *Love in the Ruins* (New York: Avon Books, 1971), 329.
4. Margaret Atwood, *Two-Headed Poems* (New York: Simon and Schuster, 1978), 85.
5. Urie Bronfenbrenner, "The Calamitous Decline of the American Family," from the Outlook section, *The Washington Post*, Sunday, January 2, 1977.
6. Peter Berger and Brigette Berger, *The War Over the Family* (New York: Doubleday, 1983), 176.
7. Carol Gilligan, "Do the Social Sciences Have an Adequate Theory of Moral Development?" in *Social Science as Moral Inquiry*, edited by Norma Haan, Robert N. Bellah, Paul Rabinow, and William M. Sullivan (New York: Columbia University Press, 1983), 47.
8. Ibid., 34.
9. Ivan Boszormenyi-Nagy and Geraldine M. Spark, *Invisible Loyalties* (Hagerstown: Harper & Row, 1973), 81.
10. Brigette Berger, "The Family as a Mediating Structure," in *Democracy and Mediating Structures*, edited by Michael Novak (Washington, D.C.: American Enterprise Institute, 1980), 144.
11. Raoul Naroll, *The Moral Order* (Beverly Hills: Sage Publications, 1983).
12. William Phipps, *Christian Century* (April 3, 1985): 327–328.
13. Craig Dykstra, *Vision and Imagination* (New York: Paulist Press, 1981), 51.
14. Elise Boulding, "Familia Farber: The Family as Maker of the Future," *Journal of Marriage and the Family* (May 1983).
15. Wendell Berry, *Standing by Words* (San Francisco: North Point Press, 1983), 73.

4. THE SMALL COMMUNITY AND THE MEDIATING SYSTEM

1. Willie Morris, "Now That I Am Fifty," *Parade Magazine* (April 21, 1985): 17.
2. Philip Slater, "Beyond Networks: Professional Conversation for the 1980's," unpublished paper, June 1982.
3. Peter Berger, Foreword, in Lowell S. Levin and Ellen L. Idler, *The Hidden Health Care System: Mediating Structures and Medicine* (Cambridge, Mass.: Ballinger Publishing, 1981), ix. See also Peter L. Berger and Richard

John Neuhaus, *To Empower People* (Washington, D.C.: American Enterprise Institute for Public Policy Research, 1977). Berger and Neuhaus talk of mediating structures. We believe that their definition significantly overlooks the interdependence of these structures, an interdependence that is so complete as to form a whole, hence the term "system."

4. Arthur Morgan, *The Small Community* (Yellow Springs, Ohio: Community Services, Inc., 1942), 57.

5. James V. Cunningham and Milton Kotler, *Building Neighborhood Organizations* (Notre Dame: University of Notre Dame Press, 1983), 3.

6. "Improvement of Quality of Life in a Neighborhood," undated and unpublished paper by the Cathedral College of the Laity, Washington, D.C.

7. Russell L. Ackoff, "Does Quality of Life Have to Be Quantified?" *Operational Research Quarterly* 27, no. 21: 299.

8. Berger and Neuhaus, *To Empower People*, 27.

9. Ibid.

10. Ibid., 30.

11. Ibid., 33.

12. Ibid., 28.

13. Ibid., 26.

14. Lyle Schaller, "The Rural Church in an Urban World," *Circuit Rider* (March 1985): 15.

15. Ibid., 17.

5. REPAIR AND TRANSFORMATION

1. See James Alexander, *The Timeless Way of Building* (New York: Oxford, 1979), 485. Alexander says that "when we repair something in the new sense, we assume that we are going to transform it, that new wholes will be born, that, indeed, the entire whole which is being repaired will become a different whole as the result of the repair" (p. 485).

2. C. Froland, D. Pancoast, N. Chapman, and P. Kimboko, *Helping Networks and Human Services* (Beverly Hills: Sage Publications, 1981), 21.

3. Daniel Goleman, "Great Altruists: Science Ponders Soul of Goodness," *New York Times* (March 5, 1985): 19.

4. Arthur Morgan, *The Small Community* (Yellow Springs, Ohio: Community Services, Inc., 1942), 19.

5. William Smart, "Trends: Uniting Against Crime," *The Washington Post* (June 14, 1984):B5, quoting Michael Castleman, *Crime Free: How to Stop Your Chances of Being Robbed, Raped, Mugged or Burglarized* (New York: Simon and Schuster, 1984).

6. Donald I. Warren, *Helping Networks* (Notre Dame: University of Notre Dame Press, 1981), 194.

7. Ibid., 8.

8. Peter Ken, "They Help People Looking for Self-help," *The New York Times*, (July 10, 1982): 46, quoting Frank Riessman. Riessman is coauthor with Alan Gartner of *Self Help in the Human Services* (San Francisco: Jossey-Bass, 1979).

9. Quoted in *Community Intervention* (Spring 1985): 8.

10. "Getting to Know Your Early Twentieth Century Neighborhood," *Conserve Neighborhoods* 25 (July–August 1982): 238–239.

11. *John Naisbitt's Trend Letter* 4, no. 8 (April 18, 1985): 3.

12. Walter Brueggeman, quoted from two lectures on vision and leadership given to the Bishops' Roundtable at the United Methodist General Board of Discipleship, Nashville, Tennessee, December 12–13, 1984.

13. Scott Peck, *The Road Less Traveled* (New York: Simon and Schuster, 1978), 39.

14. Dennis Geaney, "What Must I Be to Minister?" in *Ministering in a Servant Church*, edited by Francis A. Eigo (Villanova, Pa.: Villanova University Press, 1978), 156.

15. Tilden Edwards, *All God's Children* (Nashville: Abingdon, 1982), 109.

16. Frederick Buechner, *The Sacred Journey* (San Francisco: Harper & Row, 1982), 5.

17. Jurgen Habermas, *Legitimation Crisis*, translated by Thomas McCarthy (Boston: Beacon Press, 1973), 37.

18. George Will, *Statecraft as Soulcraft: What Government Does* (New York: Simon and Schuster, 1983), 84.

19. Amitai Etzioni, *An Immodest Agenda* (New York: McGraw-Hill, 1983), 135.

20. Buechner, *Sacred Journey*, 107.

21. Will, *Statecraft*, 81.

22. Phrase from our colleague and friend Neil Alexander.

EPILOGUE

1. Vickie Kilgore, "Intimacy, Independence Can Coexist in a Relationship," *The Tennessean*, Wednesday, April 24, 1985, 1-D.

2. Daniel Q. Haney, "Healthier Lifestyles Found Principle Factor in Reduced Heart Disease Risk," *The Tennessean* (December 26, 1984), A-10.

3. Martin Marty, *Context* 17, no. 8 (April 15, 1985): 3.

Index